D0485641

# THE MYSTERY OF ECONOMIC GROWTH

# THE MYSTERY OF
# ECONOMIC GROWTH

ELHANAN HELPMAN

THE BELKNAP PRESS OF
HARVARD UNIVERSITY PRESS
Cambridge, Massachusetts, and London, England

First Harvard University Press paperback edition, 2010

*Library of Congress Cataloging-in-Publication Data*
Helpman, Elhanan.
The mystery of economic growth / Elhanan Helpman.
p.  cm.
Includes bibliographical references and index.
ISBN 978-0-674-01572-2 (cloth : alk. paper)
ISBN 978-0-674-04605-4 (pbk.)
1. Economic development.   2. Saving and investment.
3. Production (Economic theory)   I. Title.
HD82.H435    2004
338.9—dc22    2004042217

*To Limor and Liat*
*whose miraculous growing up has been*
*a ceaseless source of joy,*
*with love*

# CONTENTS

# PREFACE

For centuries economists have been preoccupied with the growth of nations, and they have studied this subject continually since the days of Adam Smith. This effort has produced a better understanding of the sources of economic growth. But the subject has proved elusive, and many mysteries remain.

Two recent waves of research have changed our views on the subject. One wave started in the mid-1950s and lasted until the early 1970s. The second started in the mid-1980s and continues to this day. Both led to major revisions of the theory and empirics of growth. I participated as a researcher in the second wave, and I have closely followed its unfolding. This short book describes what I have learned.

This book provides a nontechnical description of growth economics in order to arrive at summary conclusions about what we know, what we do not know, and what it is that we need to learn in order to improve our understanding of a subject that affects, in major ways, the well-being of billions of people across the globe. But in undertaking this project I had no intention of writing a survey of the literature. The book presents my personal views and assessments and reflects my personal biases.

I feel that it is important to present these research findings to a broad audience, consisting of not only economists with technical expertise but also other economists, social scientists who are not economists, policymakers, and other interested readers. The subject is not only important; it is also intellectually fascinating and absorbing.

The scientific literature, consisting of both theoretical and empirical studies, is huge. Nevertheless, important messages can be extracted from this vast research, and they can be summarized and explained in (almost) plain English. Here I attempt to do just that.

My tale of growth economics is organized around four themes. First, the accumulation of physical and human capital is important, but it explains only part of the variation across countries in income per capita and its rate of growth. Technological and institutional factors also affect the rate of accumulation of these capital inputs, and they are in some sense more fundamental. Second, total factor productivity is at least as important as accumulation. (For a brief explanation of total factor productivity and other economic terms, see the Glossary.) To understand its determinants we need to understand what shapes the accumulation of knowledge and, in particular, the incentives for knowledge creation. This leads us naturally to explore the effects of research and development, learning-by-doing, externalities, and increasing returns. It also leads us to examine the institutional factors that encourage or discourage knowledge creation. Third, growth rates of different countries are interdependent, because knowledge flows across national borders, and foreign trade and investment affect the incentives to innovate, to imitate, and to use new technologies. Fourth, economic and political institutions affect the incentives to accumulate and to innovate, and they also affect the ability of countries to accommodate change.

A recent surge of research on the effects of institutions and politics on economic growth has convincingly shown the importance of these elements of social structures. But as of now, we understand these channels of influence less well than some of the others discussed in this book. If I were to write this book five years from today, I probably would write the same book except for the chapter on institutions and politics, because I believe that much progress will be made in this area in the next few years.

Since this is not a survey, I have omitted certain topics from my story. Important among them is endogenous population growth. The omission of a topic, however, does not imply that I consider it to be unimportant. Rather it implies that—on the basis of my understanding of the literature—I am not able to coherently fit the topic into my tale. Part of this reflects my ignorance. Another part reflects my differences of opinion with other scholars. To all those who labor on topics that I have ignored, my apologies.

I have been fortunate to be a member of the Economic Growth and Policy Program and the Institutions, Organizations and Economic Growth Program of the Canadian Institute for Advanced Research (CIAR). This unique Canadian institution has given me the opportunity to study economic growth for a prolonged period of time, and in the process to interact with some of the world's most distinguished scholars. My participation in these programs has been an intellectual feast, where true scholarship has been practiced with comradeship and zeal. Fraser

Mustard, the founder of the CIAR, is a man of vision and a great believer in the power of ideas. His initial support of the unorthodox approach to economic growth taken by myself and others was critical for the launching of our first program. In addition, I would like to thank the National Science Foundation for its support of my research.

The epigraph is reprinted from the *Journal of Monetary Economics*, 22, Robert E. Lucas, Jr., "On the Mechanics of Economic Development," p. 5, copyright 1988, with permission from Elsevier.

I have also been blessed with friends and colleagues who took the time to read the manuscript and who gave me wise advice on a host of issues. They saved me from errors and encouraged me to carry on with this project. They are Daron Acemoglu, Philippe Aghion, Alberto Alesina, Pol Antràs, Michael Aronson, Francesco Caselli, Zvi Eckstein, Harry Flam, Oded Galor, Avner Greif, Gene Grossman, Peter Howitt, Dale Jorgenson, Lawrence Katz, Torsten Persson, Assaf Razin, Kenneth Shepsle, Andrei Shleifer, Guido Tabellini, Manuel Trajtenberg, and Daniel Trefler. Although I did not always follow their advice, I always carefully considered their suggestions. For their contributions to this book I will remain forever grateful.

Finally, my gratitude to Jane Trahan for editing the manuscript. She patiently converted Hebrew-tainted verses into proper English.

The consequences for human welfare involved in questions like these are simply staggering: Once one starts to think about them, it is hard to think about anything else.

Robert E. Lucas, Jr.

# 1

## BACKGROUND

What makes some countries rich and others poor? Economists have asked this question since the days of Adam Smith. Yet after more than two hundred years, the mystery of economic growth has not been solved.

Living standards differ greatly across countries. So do the rates at which these standards change. Some countries grow richer quickly, others slowly. And in some of the poorest nations the standard of living has declined over prolonged periods of time.

Economists use real income per capita to measure how well off people are. Obviously, people care about income. But they also care about other issues, such as political freedom, education, health, the environment, and the degree of inequality in their societies. For this reason a good measure of living standards has to account for many factors. But most of them are hard to measure. And it is even harder to decide how much weight to give each one. As a result, real income per capita is often used as a rough measure of a country's standard of living.[1]

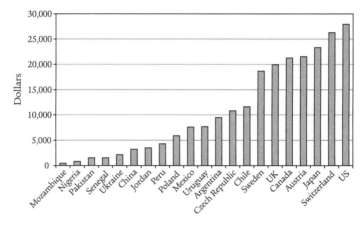

**Figure 1.1** Real GNP per capita, 1996. Data from Summers and Heston, PWT 5.6.

Today income per capita differs across countries much more than it used to. Such differences were small up until the nineteenth century. They started to widen with the Industrial Revolution, and they expanded most during the last hundred years.[2] Moreover, although differences in income per capita among rich countries have declined in the post–World War II period, the disparity between rich and poor countries has widened. At the same time, the number of middle-income countries has dwindled. We now have two polarized economic clubs: one rich, the other poor.[3]

Figure 1.1 describes income per capita in a sample of countries.[4] It demonstrates the disparities that existed in 1996. In that year income per capita in Canada was more than twice as high as in Argentina and about thirteen times higher than in Pakistan. Even larger gaps existed between Canada and a number of African countries. Canada's income was, for example, about forty-

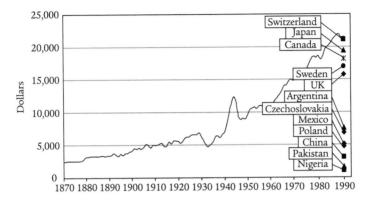

**Figure 1.2** Real GNP per capita in 1992 compared with the historical record of the United States. Data from Maddison (1995).

three times higher than Mozambique's. And Canada was not the richest country in 1996. These differences are mind boggling.

Another measure of income disparity is displayed in Figure 1.2. It depicts the real income per capita of thirteen countries in 1992. One of them is the United States, for which the figure also shows the evolution of income since 1870. We can pick out from this figure the years in which the United States had the same income level as each one of the remaining countries had in 1992. According to these data, in 1992 Argentina's income per capita was comparable to the income per capita of the United States around World War II, while Pakistan's was lower than U.S. income in 1870. These very long lags suggest that it will take many years before Argentina and Pakistan catch up to the current standard of living in the United States.

Economic growth is measured by the rate of change of real income per capita. A country with a growth rate of 1 percent per

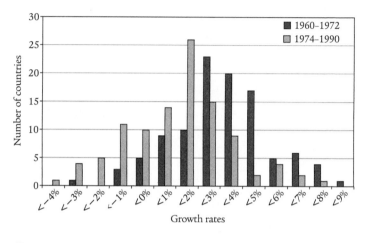

**Figure 1.3**  Average annual growth rates of real GDP per capita: 104 countries. Data from Summers and Heston, PWT 5.6.

annum doubles its living standard every seventy years, while a country with a growth rate of 3 percent doubles its living standard every twenty-three years. It follows that prolonged differences in growth rates produce dramatic differences in living standards.

Indeed, growth rates have differed greatly across countries. Figure 1.3 summarizes the frequency distribution of the growth rates of 104 countries during three decades in the post–World War II era, from 1960 to 1990.[5] I have divided these decades into two periods, one prior to the oil crisis of 1973 and one following the oil crisis: 1960–1972 and 1974–1990. The figure shows that more countries experienced higher growth rates before the oil crisis than after it. In the first period no country experienced an average decline of income per capita that exceeded 4 percent per year and only one country had an average decline between 3 percent and 4 percent (Burundi). In the second period, however, one country had a rate of decline in excess of 4 percent (Nicaragua) and four countries had a rate of decline between 3 percent and 4 percent. More generally, in every growth bracket below 2 percent there were more countries in the latter period while in every growth bracket above 2 percent there were more countries in the former period. The simple average rate of growth of the 104 countries was 3.0 percent in the former period; it dropped to 1.1 percent in the latter. Moreover, the coefficient of variation of these growth rates—calculated with equal weights for every country—increased from 0.733 in the former period to 2.091 in the latter.[6] The disparity in rates of growth has clearly grown.

Although negative developments also afflicted the sample's 21 richest economies in the post–oil crisis period, the decline in their average growth rates was smaller and they did not experience a rise in disparity.[7] Figure 1.4 depicts the frequency distribution of growth rates in these economies. Their average growth rate declined from 4 percent per annum to 2 percent. But in each period it was higher than the average growth rate for the larger sample of 104 countries, which was 3.0 percent and 1.1 percent, respectively, in the two periods. The average growth rate of the rich countries declined by a factor of two, while in the larger sample it declined by a factor of three. Finally, the coefficient of variation of the growth rates of the rich countries was 0.35 in both periods, while it increased by a factor of three (from 0.733 to 2.091) in the larger group.

An important difference between the rich and poor countries is that even after the worldwide slowdown in economic growth that followed the oil crisis, none of the rich countries experienced a prolonged period of declining income per capita. The story was different for the poor countries in the larger sample.

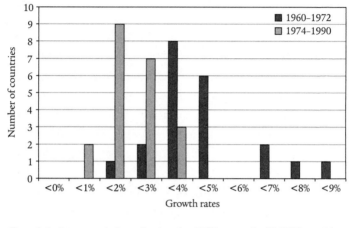

**Figure 1.4**  Average annual growth rates of real GDP per capita: 21 OECD countries.
Data from Summers and Heston, PWT 5.6.

Figure 1.3 indicates that while prior to the oil crisis only nine countries had negative growth rates, afterward that number increased to thirty-two. This group includes Angola, Chad, Haiti, Mali, and Somalia, in which the standard of living deteriorated by frightening proportions.[8]

Despite the volatility of the post–World War II period, it has been a time of remarkable growth. Maddison (2001) provides estimates of economic growth for the longest span of time. His estimates of the average rate of growth of income per capita for the world economy are presented in Figure 1.5. According to these data, growth was negligible from the Middle Ages to the Industrial Revolution, and it picked up in earnest only in the nineteenth century. From the early part of the nineteenth century until World War I growth accelerated dramatically. World War I, the Great Depression between the wars, and World War II slowed

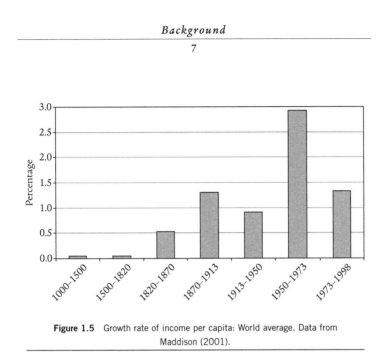

**Figure 1.5** Growth rate of income per capita: World average. Data from Maddison (2001).

down growth. But even during those years of upheaval growth remained high by historical standards. World War II was followed by the Golden Age of economic growth, a period of rapid expansion not matched by any other historical episode.[9] The Golden Age lasted until the early 1970s. With the outbreak of the oil crisis in 1973, economic growth slowed down. Nevertheless, judged by historical standards, growth remained high even after the oil crisis.

To summarize, average income per capita has grown significantly since World War II, and at a high rate by historical standards. Growth rates have been uneven, however, and the disparity in income per capita between rich and poor countries has increased. In order to understand these developments we need to identify forces of convergence, which have induced countries with low income per capita to catch up with the rich countries, and forces of divergence, which have induced rich countries to forge even further ahead of the poor countries. And we also need to understand why average income per capita has grown overall, and at an accelerated rate in recent decades.

# 2

## ACCUMULATION

We have seen that the average income per capita of many countries has grown substantially in the post–World War II period, but that national growth rates were very uneven, high in some countries and negative in others. The question is, Why? Or more precisely, What mechanisms drove these large improvements in the standard of living? And why did they work to the benefit of some countries but not others?

Macroeconomists have emphasized the accumulation of physical and human capital as major forces behind income growth. Physical capital consists of the stock of machines, equipment, and structures, while human capital consists of the stock of education and training embodied in the labor force. Accumulation of these factors was thought to respond to economic incentives, which is why they have gained center stage in the analysis of economic growth. The same macroeconomists treated technological change as an exogenous process, however, that is, as one outside the influence of economic incentives. As a result, they paid only rudimentary attention to technological change.

Following this tradition, I discuss in this chapter the contribution of factor accumulation to economic growth, treating technological change as an exogenous process. In the next chapter I show, however, that productivity is even more important than these factors in explaining income differences and growth rate differences across countries. Motivated by this evidence, I will examine the possibility that technological change may be endogenous, and I will discuss that and other determinants of productivity levels in Chapter 4.

## Capital Accumulation

The main insights about the effects of capital accumulation on growth are due to Solow (1956, 1957), who is the founder of the neoclassical growth model. They can be summarized with the aid of Figure 2.1, in which the horizontal axis represents the economy's capital intensity, defined as the ratio of capital to effective labor. Effective labor is measured in efficiency units. It is the product of labor hours and a measure of the productivity of labor.

The vertical axis represents both the ratio of saving to effective labor and the ratio of the replacement requirement to effective labor. Superimposing two coordinate systems like this allows us to depict not only the relationship of each of these ratios to capital intensity but also their relationship to each other. One curve describes saving per effective unit of labor. In this model aggregate saving equals a constant fraction of income. The curve is concave, because—due to the declining marginal productivity of capital—the adding of a unit of capital adds less to output the larger the capital stock. The ray through the origin describes the investment in capital per effective unit of labor that is needed to keep the capital-labor ratio at its original level, assuming that

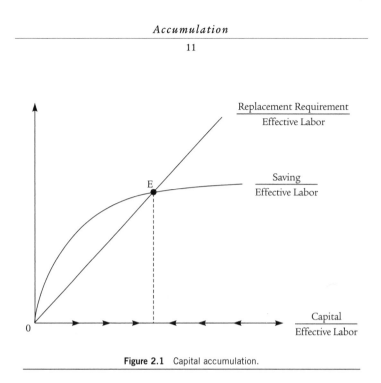

**Figure 2.1** Capital accumulation.

the population grows at a constant rate, that capital depreciates at a constant rate, and that labor productivity improves at a constant rate. The required investment compensates the capital stock for population growth, capital depreciation, and technological progress. A larger population supplies more working hours. As a result, the capital intensity would decline if the capital stock were to remain constant. Investment is needed to restore the original capital intensity. Depreciation reduces the capital stock. Therefore investment is needed to restore the original capital stock and the original capital intensity. And, finally, technological progress that raises the productivity of workers expands the effective supply of labor. If the stock of capital did not change, the capital-labor ratio would decline. Therefore, again, investment is needed to restore the original capital intensity.

Whenever saving exceeds the replacement requirement, investment exceeds the amount needed to maintain constant capital intensity. As a result, the capital-labor ratio rises. But when saving falls short of the replacement requirement, the ratio of capital to effective labor declines. The arrows on the horizontal axis show the implied directions of change in capital intensity. A long-run equilibrium is attained when saving equals the required replacement. Such an equilibrium is depicted by point E, where the two curves intersect.

Solow developed his theory in order to explain the effect of capital accumulation on the growth of a single country. Nevertheless, his framework has been repeatedly used to compare growth trajectories of different countries. To make such comparisons, one assumes that Figure 2.1 applies to every country in the sample.[1] Under the circumstances, capital intensity rises in countries with capital-labor ratios to the left of the long-run equilibrium point, and so does output per effective unit of labor.[2] Since labor productivity rises as well, output per capita grows.[3] In the long run, the capital intensity stabilizes. As a result, output per effective unit of labor stabilizes as well. It then follows that output per worker grows at a constant rate, which equals the rate of technological progress. During the transition to the long-run equilibrium, however, the rate of growth of output per capita declines. It starts higher than the rate of technological progress and it gradually declines to the rate of technological progress.

Countries with capital intensity to the right of point E save less than is necessary to preserve their capital intensity. As a result, in every such country the capital intensity declines. The decline in capital intensity proceeds until it reaches its long-run equilibrium level. During the transition, the growth rate of output per capita converges to the rate of technological progress.[4]

Two important features of accumulation-driven growth emerge from this discussion. First, the growth rate of income per capita converges to the rate of technological progress in the long run. Since the rate of technological progress has been assumed to be constant, however, this implies that the long-run rate of growth cannot be affected by the state of the economy or by economic incentives.[5]

Second, growth rates vary with capital intensity: the growth rate of income per capita is lower the higher the capital-labor ratio. This has two implications: (a) the growth rate of a country declines over time when its capital intensity rises, and its growth rate rises over time when its capital intensity declines; and (b) in a cross-country comparison, countries with higher capital intensity grow more slowly.

How well does this model explain the data? I will discuss parts of the evidence in this chapter and other parts in the next.

## Convergence

The negative relationship between the growth rate of output per capita and the initial capital-labor ratio—a key implication of Solow's model—has been empirically examined in many studies. King and Rebelo (1993) provide one example.[6] They analyzed the evolution of the U.S. economy over the course of one hundred years, when income per capita increased sevenfold. They asked whether transitional dynamics driven by capital accumulation could explain this rise, and concluded that it could not explain even half. Calibration of the model to the data implied, for example, unreasonably high marginal productivity levels of capital in the early phases. These would have implied in turn real interest rates in excess of 100 percent, far above the real interest rates in the data. Various modifications to deal with this counterfactual implication produced other inconsistencies.

Unlike this study, many others have looked for evidence regarding Solow's model in cross-country correlations between capital intensities and growth rates of output per capita. Since output per capita is an increasing function of capital intensity and data on output per capita are more reliable and more available than data on capital intensity, those studies examined the correlation between initial levels of output per capita and its subsequent growth. Controlling for variables that affect steady states, they found a negative correlation, consistent with the theory. Barro and Sala-i-Martin (1992) named this finding *conditional convergence*. It is one of the most robust relationships in these data.

Cross-country variations in rates of saving and population growth generate differences in long-run capital intensities. On the one hand, it can be shown with the aid of Figure 2.1 that a higher saving rate accelerates the short-run rate of per capita income growth and raises the long-run capital intensity. On the other hand, higher population growth reduces the short-run rate of growth and the long-run capital intensity. For these reasons estimates of conditional convergence need to control for cross-country variations in saving rates and rates of population growth. These studies did control for such variations, but they assumed that the shape of the production function and the rate of technological change were the same in all countries.

Barro and Sala-i-Martin (1992) found that income per capita converged to its long-run value at a rate of about 2 percent per annum.[7] That is, about 2 percent of the gap between the initial income per capita and its long-run value is closed every year. This represents a very slow transition to the long-run equilibrium.[8] The magnitude of this rate of convergence is closely related to the elasticity of output with respect to the capital stock, which measures how readily output changes when the capital stock changes. The higher this elasticity, the faster the transition.

Barro and Sala-i-Martin pointed out that while the data support the hypothesis of conditional convergence, they do not support the hypothesis of convergence that is not conditioned on steady states, that is, the hypothesis of *unconditional convergence.* Their findings are consistent with the evidence from the previous chapter, where it was shown that incomes per capita in a large sample of countries have not converged in the post–World War II period. There is evidence of convergence within the group of rich countries, but not across the groups of rich and poor countries.

These results pose the following question: What are the forces of divergence in the world economy? If incomes per capita were driven by capital accumulation and a common rate of technological progress only, then growth rates between the poor and the rich countries would have converged. The reason is that capital is more productive in the capital-scarce countries, which are poor, thereby providing an incentive for faster capital accumulation in the developing part of the world. As a result, their income per capita should have grown faster. But it has not. This means that other factors must have played a major role in shaping patterns of growth.

One may suspect that the absence from this discussion of an explicit role for human capital accumulation is responsible for the gap between this theory and the data. It is not. I will discuss the evidence on human capital at a later stage. Here let me point out only that, as long as the accumulation of human capital is also subject to declining marginal productivity, its inclusion does not change the basic predictions. Countries with lower human and physical capital, where capital is more productive, should grow faster than countries with more highly educated workers and larger stocks of physical capital. And in the long run, the rate of growth of income per capita should equal the rate of technological progress. In these circumstances conditional convergence would still hold. As a result, we would still expect the gap between the poor and rich countries to close over time.[9] Lack of convergence therefore suggests that accumulation is not the dominant force.

Convergence of income per capita as a result of capital accumulation should have been particularly strong after 1980, when international capital mobility began to expand rapidly.[10] With the removal of barriers to the international flow of capital, investors find it much easier to seek out countries with high returns to capital and to invest in them. Since countries with low capital-labor ratios have high returns to capital, they should attract foreign investment from the rich countries, whose capital intensity is high. But we do not observe large flows of capital from rich to poor countries. In fact, most of the international capital flows—in the form of foreign direct investment and portfolio investment—take place within the group of rich countries. It therefore must be that either the productivity of capital is not particularly high in the less-developed countries, the risk of investing in those countries is much higher than the risk of investing in the rich countries, or the Solow model does not provide an adequate framework for dealing with these issues.[11]

Lucas (1990) made a forceful argument. He pointed out that in 1985 the United States had an income per capita that was fifteen times higher than in India. Had this difference been the result of differences in capital intensity only, the rate of return on capital in India should have been fifty-eight times higher than in the United States. With such a large difference in rates of return,

U.S. investors should have moved funds to India en masse. But on the contrary, no large capital flows from the United States to India were recorded at that time.

Lucas thought that quality differences between Indian and American workers might be affecting the numbers. When he made corrections for differences in human capital, however, the gap between the rates of return on physical capital shrank, but did not disappear. Using estimates from Krueger (1968), Lucas calculated that an American worker was five times more productive than an Indian worker. Therefore, measured in capital per effective unit of labor, the corrected U.S. capital intensity was only one-fifth of the original estimate. As a result the corrected rate of return to capital in India was only five times higher than in the United States. A much smaller gap, to be sure, but still large enough to trigger major capital flows, which did not take place. The puzzle persisted.

## Differences in Income per Capita

Mankiw, Romer, and Weil (1992) examined another implication of Solow's model. They assumed that all countries have the same Cobb-Douglas production function, the same rate of technological change, and the same rate of capital depreciation. With these assumptions they showed that the cross-country variation in income per capita is a simple function of the cross-country variation in the rate of saving, the rate of population growth, and the initial level of labor productivity. Assuming, in addition, that every country is in its long-run equilibrium and that initial differences in the logarithm of labor productivity are randomly distributed across countries allowed Mankiw, Romer, and Weil to estimate this equation.

Their estimates explain about 60 percent of the 1985 cross-country variation in income per capita for a mixed sample of ninety-eight non–oil producing developed and developing countries.[12] However, when they recovered the implied share of capital in national income from these estimates, they found it to be almost twice as large as direct estimates of the capital share.

To deal with this discrepancy, Mankiw, Romer, and Weil added human capital accumulation to their model. Parallel to the accumulation of physical capital, they assumed that a fixed fraction of income was spent on investment in human capital. They used the secondary school enrollment rate in the working-age population as a proxy for the fraction of income invested in human capital. With these modifications, the estimated equation explains close to 80 percent of the 1985 cross-country variation in income per capita. Importantly, the share of physical capital in income that is recovered from these estimates equals 31 percent, which is close to the directly computed capital share.

Mankiw, Romer, and Weil concluded that their modified version of Solow's model, which accounts for the accumulation of physical and human capital, explains the data well. This position was echoed in Mankiw (1995). Should we accept this view and conclude that this model provides a satisfactory explanation of economic growth? I do not think so, and I explain why in the next chapter.

# 3

## PRODUCTIVITY

**P**roductivity is an elusive concept. It is used to describe a variety of characteristics that affect the relationship between inputs and outputs. I use, for example, a coefficient that converts labor hours into effective labor units to measure *labor productivity*. *Labor-augmenting* technological change is represented by the growth of this coefficient.

Technological change need not be labor augmenting, however. It can also be capital augmenting or land augmenting. That is, improvements in technology can enhance the productivity of labor, capital, or land, and they can enhance the productivity of various inputs to different degrees.

In addition to these input-biased productivity improvements, technological change can raise output by a factor of proportionality that is independent of the composition of inputs employed in production. This type of proportional shift is called *Hicks-neutral* technological change. To illustrate, suppose that there is a 3 percent Hicks-neutral improvement in productivity. Then a combination of inputs that used to produce 1 trillion dollars of output at constant prices now produces 1.03 trillion dollars of output. And a combination of inputs that was capable of producing 400 million dollars' worth of output, now produces 412 million dollars. And these output changes do not depend on the inputs used to produce the 1 trillion or 400 million dollars' worth of output.

Finally, economists use the concept of *total factor productivity (TFP)* to measure the joint effectiveness of all inputs combined in producing output. Changes in TFP, which are separate from changes in inputs, represent the joint effects of all input-augmenting technological improvements and the effect of Hicks-neutral technological change.[1]

Having multiple concepts of productivity requires some care in the use of this term. Such care is not always exercised, however. The term "labor productivity" is often used to describe output per worker or output per hour, rather than the labor-augmenting productivity measure. It also is common to use the term "productivity" as a shorthand for "labor productivity." To avoid confusion, I will refer to the productivity of an input as the size of the coefficient that converts natural units of the input, such as hours of labor or acres of land, into effective units of the input. Growth in the productivity of an input will therefore refer to growth of this productivity coefficient, in line with the discussion in the previous chapter.

How can we measure the extent to which inputs have become more productive? The answer depends on how narrowly we define inputs and on how carefully we specify the production relationships. As an example, consider labor. Some workers have only a primary school education, others have a secondary school education, and still others have college degrees. An hour of work of a college graduate is, of course, not identical to an hour of work of a high school dropout. And the contribution to output of each one of them depends on her job. Experience may also be important. A worker with ten years of experience is typically more productive than a worker with only one year of experience. For this reason the aggregation of all working hours into a single measure of labor input, without accounting for differences in education and experience, does not provide an accurate measure of labor input. To convert these hours into effective labor units, we need to design a labor productivity measure that accounts for the heterogeneity of the labor force. The correction of employment for education and experience creates a measure of *human capital*. But these corrections may not be enough to fully reflect changes in labor productivity, because changes in technology or in workplace organization can further improve the productivity of workers.

As with labor inputs, capital inputs also need adjustment for quality. Drilling machines that were produced in 1950 do not yield the same services as drilling machines that were produced in 1990. And changes in technology and the organization of work affect to different degrees the productivity of machines of different types, ages, and qualities.

## Growth Accounting

Economists have been measuring the contribution of inputs to output growth for many years. An elaborate methodology, known as "growth accounting," has developed for this purpose. Solow (1957) provided the most important early contribution.[2]

The central idea behind growth accounting is that the growth of output can be decomposed, or broken down, into components that can be attributed to the growth of inputs and a residual growth rate that is not attributed to the growth of inputs. The rate of growth of output that is attributed to a particular input equals the input's share in GDP multiplied by the rate of growth of the input.[3] Thus the contribution of all inputs combined equals a weighted average of the growth rates of inputs, in which the weight of every input equals its share in GDP. As an example, suppose that the labor share is 60 percent and the capital share is 40 percent. Also suppose that labor hours grow at 2 percent per annum and the capital stock grows at 1 percent per annum. Then the contribution of these inputs to output growth is 1.6 percent.

As it happens, the contribution of inputs to output growth does not necessarily equal the rate of output growth. In a typical data set the growth of output exceeds the contribution of inputs. The difference between the rate of growth of output and the contribution of input growth represents the rate of growth of total factor productivity. That is, it represents the aggregate effect of the various forms of technological change. If, for example, output growth were 4 percent in the numerical example from the previous paragraph, it would imply TFP growth of 2.4 percent. So in this example the output growth of 4 percent is decomposed into a 1.6 percent growth rate attributable to the growth of inputs and a 2.4 percent growth rate of TFP. It is customary to describe the ratio of the growth rate of TFP to the growth rate of output as the fraction of growth that is "explained" by TFP growth. In the example this fraction is 0.6. That is, 60 percent of the growth rate is due to productivity improvements.

How much output growth is attributed by growth accounting to improvements in TFP and how much to the growth of inputs depends, however, on the ways in which the input measures are constructed. If, for example, labor input is measured in hours, unadjusted for education and experience, then in an economy with rising average years of schooling the contribution of schooling to the quality of the labor force will be attributed to TFP growth. Similarly, if the measured stock of capital does not account for quality improvements, the contribution of a rising quality of capital will be attributed to TFP growth. More generally, all unmeasured improvements in the quality of inputs—improvements in technology, improvements in the organization of production and distribution, the reduction of distortions (harmful regulations or taxes), and improvements in government policies—will be attributed to TFP growth.

Solow (1957) calculated TFP growth in the U.S. nonfarm private sector for the first half of the twentieth century. He found it to be close to 80 percent of the rate of output growth. According to this measure, an increase in TFP was the overwhelming source of U.S. growth. Solow did not account for improvements in the quality of inputs, however. Such improvements were introduced by other researchers. Dale Jorgenson was instrumental in improving the construction of quality-adjusted input variables, beginning with the Jorgenson and Griliches (1967) study. These improvements have substantially reduced the measured contribution of TFP to output growth. Nevertheless, TFP has remained a major source of growth, even in countries with the finest quality adjustments.

Figure 3.1 shows the ratio of TFP growth to output growth in the world's seven largest economies—the G7—over the 1960–1995 period. The estimates of TFP and output growth are from Jorgenson and Yip (2001, tables 12.4 and 12.6), who used quality-adjusted capital stocks and labor inputs. Despite their careful adjustments, close to 50 percent of Japanese output growth and

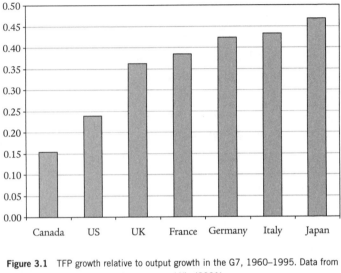

**Figure 3.1** TFP growth relative to output growth in the G7, 1960–1995. Data from Jorgenson and Yip (2001).

more than 40 percent of German and Italian output growth are attributed to TFP growth, indicating that it was important for the growth of their output. Canada had the slowest pace of productivity improvement and the contribution of its TFP to output growth was the smallest, only 15 percent of the total. These fractions are much smaller than the 80 percent found by Solow, but they are substantial nevertheless.[4]

Another set of careful calculations was done by Young (1995) for the four East Asian newly industrialized countries (NICs)—Hong Kong, Taiwan, Korea, and Singapore—over the 1966–1990 period.[5] For these countries the ratio of TFP growth to output growth is presented in Figure 3.2. Labor force participation increased substantially during those years and in some of the countries high saving rates led to fast accumulation of capital,

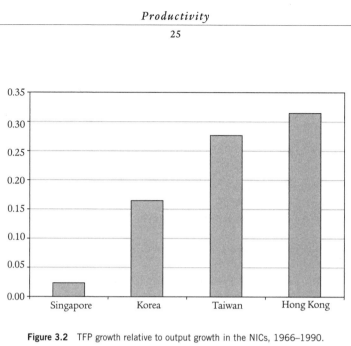

**Figure 3.2**  TFP growth relative to output growth in the NICs, 1966–1990.
Data from Young (1995).

an input. Taking account of these trends and adjusting inputs for quality improvements, Young found that only in Singapore was TFP growth extremely small. In Korea TFP growth accounted for 16 percent of output growth, in Taiwan it accounted for 27 percent, and in Hong Kong for 31 percent. The rest of the output growth was attributed to accumulation. These findings led Krugman (1994) to argue that the miracle rates of output growth that existed in these countries were not sustainable, because growth that is driven by accumulation has to decline due to the declining marginal productivity of capital.[6]

## Causality

Although growth accounting decomposes output growth into the contribution of inputs and the contribution of total factor productivity,[7] it does not unveil the *causes* of economic growth. This important point is often overlooked.

Consider, for example, Korea, in which the rate of TFP growth was 16 percent of the rate of output growth between 1960 and 1990 (see Figure 3.2). One may be tempted to conclude from this figure that TFP played a minor role in Korea's growth process, and that the accumulation of inputs—and in particular of capital—was the main engine of growth. True, Korea had a large saving rate and it invested at extremely high rates. But these investment rates responded at least partially to the evolution of productivity. High productivity makes investment more profitable. Therefore high productivity *induces* capital accumulation. As a result, fast accumulation of capital is often a reflection of high TFP, or an expected high rate of productivity growth. Part of the output growth that is attributed to capital is, in fact, driven by productivity growth. In other words, productivity—not capital accumulation—should be credited with this fraction of output growth.

To illustrate, consider a Solow-type economy, discussed in the last chapter, in which the population is not growing and the rate of technological change equals zero. Suppose the economy is in a steady state, that is, the capital stock is constant and the capital-labor ratio is at a level that equates saving with the required replacement of capital.

Now suppose that the economy experiences an instant once-and-for-all Hicks-neutral productivity improvement of 2 percent. That is, it becomes more productive by 2 percent, but no further productivity gains take place. Solow's model predicts that under these circumstances the capital stock will gradually rise to a new steady-state level. In the new steady state, output will be higher due both to the 2 percent productivity improvement and to the accumulation of capital. Note, however, that in the absence of a productivity improvement no accumulation of capital would have taken place. Therefore one may argue that in this example the entire growth of output should be attributed to productivity growth. Growth accounting, however, would attribute part of the growth of output to capital accumulation.[8]

The causal relation between productivity and investment illustrated by this example is important not only for a proper accounting of the sources of economic growth, but also for the statistical estimation of equations that explain income per capita. Mankiw, Romer, and Weil (1992) provide an illustration. They assumed for estimation purposes that all countries had the same productivity trend, so that TFP grew at the same rate in all of them. They also assumed that the initial *levels* of TFP differed across countries, but only by a random factor that was not correlated with investment. These assumptions helped them to identify the coefficients of an equation that explains 80 percent of the cross-country variation in income per capita. On the basis of this finding, they concluded that a simple Solow-type model with a common rate of TFP growth provides a satisfactory explanation of the variation of income per capita across countries.

But Grossman and Helpman (1994a) argued that these assumptions are too restrictive, and that they bias the estimates in a systematic way. They first pointed out that the rates of TFP growth differed across countries, contrary to the Mankiw, Romer, and Weil assumption.[9] Then they showed that the rate of TFP growth and the investment-to-GDP ratio were positively correlated in a sample of twenty-two countries over the period 1970–1988.[10] This correlation biases the Mankiw, Romer, and Weil estimates, because "if investment rates are high where productivity grows fast, the coefficient on the investment variable will pick up not only the variation in per capita income due to differences in countries' tastes for savings, but also part of the variation due to their different experiences with technological progress" (Grossman and Helpman 1994a, 29). In other words, in the presence of this correlation, estimates of the cross-country variation in income per capita or the growth rate of income per capita attribute to investment more explanatory power than it deserves.

A similar insight arises from the work of Islam (1995). Like Mankiw, Romer, and Weil, he also assumed that the rate of TFP growth was common to all countries. But unlike them, he allowed the initial levels of TFP to differ. Estimating the TFP levels jointly with the income per capita equation, he found substantial variation in TFP levels across countries. His results attribute the cross-country differences in income per capita mostly to variations in TFP levels, and much less to variations in investment rates.[11]

## Productivity Differences

I have noted that productivity levels vary across countries. By how much they vary can be seen in Figure 3.3, which shows the 1960–1985 average productivity levels of fourteen countries relative to Somalia, out of a sample of ninety-six countries for which Islam (1995) provided estimates.[12] Somalia was chosen as the benchmark because it had the lowest TFP level. The variations are huge. Sweden, for example, was twenty times more productive than Somalia; Hong Kong was forty times more productive. Although estimates of this sort have to be treated with caution, they do reveal the large variations in productivity levels that exist across countries.

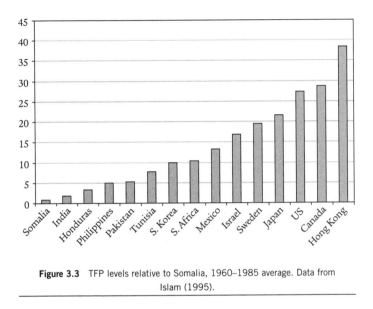

**Figure 3.3** TFP levels relative to Somalia, 1960–1985 average. Data from Islam (1995).

Islam did not control for differences in education, however. For this reason his estimates of TFP partly reflect differences in the quality of the labor force. Nevertheless, his estimates are highly correlated with the TFP estimates of Hall and Jones (1999), who did account for differences in education. In particular, the Spearman rank correlation coefficient of the two sets of estimates equals 0.9, which is very high (see Islam 2001).[13] Yet the estimated relative productivity levels differ substantially for some countries. An extreme example is Jordan, for which Islam's estimate is 25 percent of U.S. productivity while Hall and Jones's estimate is about 120 percent of U.S. productivity. These differences notwithstanding, both sets of estimates show large cross-country variations in TFP.

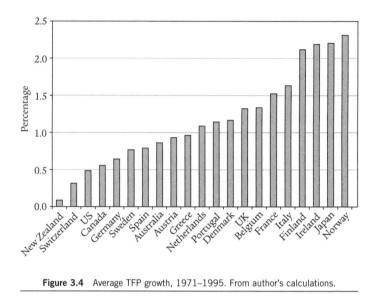

**Figure 3.4** Average TFP growth, 1971–1995. From author's calculations.

Not only do TFP levels differ across countries, but so do rates of TFP growth. This fact is illustrated in Figure 3.4 for twenty-one rich countries.[14] While Norway and Japan experienced growth of TFP in excess of 2 percent per annum, New Zealand and Switzerland had growth rates below 0.5 percent.

Another interesting fact concerns the relationship between TFP and income per capita. Figure 3.5 depicts this relationship for the ninety-six countries in Islam's sample. It is apparent that the two are positively correlated. Countries that had high levels of average TFP in the 1960–1985 period also had high income per capita in 1990. The same relationship was found between average TFP levels in 1960–1985 and income per capita in 1960.[15] In other words, rich countries are highly productive; poor countries are not. Since rich countries also have more capital per

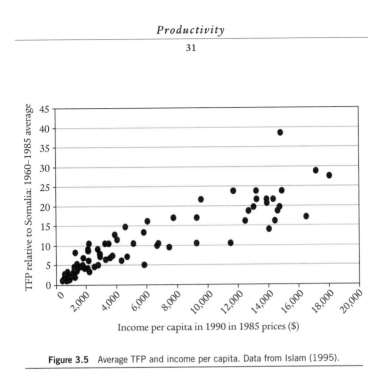

**Figure 3.5** Average TFP and income per capita. Data from Islam (1995).

worker and their workers are better educated, it follows that their income per capita is higher for all three reasons: more capital, more human capital, and higher productivity.

## Sources of Income Variation

Rich countries have an advantage in all three major determinants of income per capita. But how important is the variation in inputs as opposed to productivity in explaining the cross-country variation in the level of income per capita and the growth rate of income per capita?

Hall and Jones (1999) provide a telling illustration. In their data, income per worker is thirty-five times higher in the United States than in Niger. But the difference in capital intensity explains a ratio of only 1.5, while the difference in education levels explains a ratio of 3.1. It follows from this calculation that differences in inputs explain an output-per-worker ratio of about 4.7. TFP differences explain the residual ratio, which equals 7.7. Evidently the difference in productivity is much more important than the differences in capital and education in explaining the poor performance of Niger relative to the United States.

Is this example representative? The answer is yes. Klenow and Rodríguez-Clare (1997) decomposed the cross-country variation in income per worker into fractions that can be attributed to differences in physical capital, human capital, and TFP. The decomposition proved to be sensitive to the ways in which education was measured. In particular, Klenow and Rodríguez-Clare argued that using secondary school enrollment rates as proxies for human capital leads to an exaggeration of the role of education in explaining differences in income per worker, because secondary school enrollment rates vary across countries much more than other sensible measures of human capital. As a result, they argued, Mankiw, Romer, and Weil (1992)—who used secondary school enrollment rates—attributed too much explanatory power to human capital and too little to TFP. Adding, for example, primary school enrollment rates to secondary school enrollment rates in the construction of the human capital index significantly reduces the variation in human capital across countries, thereby reducing the prominence of human capital and raising the prominence of TFP in explaining differences in income per capita. A further shift of explanatory power from human capital to TFP occurs when human capital is measured as an aggregate of all three enrollment rates: primary, secondary, and tertiary.

Klenow and Rodríguez-Clare also constructed estimates of human capital from average years of schooling and the effects of schooling on earnings.[16] They then recalculated the decomposition of the cross-country variation in income per worker into fractions that are attributable to physical capital, human capital, and TFP. And they found that in this case too, differences in TFP play a large role in explaining differences in income. It follows from their study that all sensible measures of human capital lead to the same conclusion: more than 60 percent of the variation in income per worker is explained by differences in TFP. The role of TFP is even bigger in explaining the cross-country differences in the *growth rate* of income per worker rather than the differences in the *level* of income per worker. In the former case differences in TFP account for about 90 percent of the variation.[17]

To summarize, there is convincing evidence that total factor productivity plays a major role in accounting for the observed cross-country variation in income per worker and patterns of economic growth. We therefore need to understand what drives the differences in total factor productivity. The next chapter examines one possible answer.

# 4

## INNOVATION

We have seen that living standards vary greatly across countries, and that rich countries have higher levels of income per capita because they have more capital per worker, more educated workers, and higher levels of TFP. Importantly, more than half of the variation in income per capita results from differences in TFP. And the same applies to differences in growth rates of income per capita: more than half of the variation results from differences in TFP growth. Students of economic growth have concluded from this evidence that, in order to understand the growth of nations, it is necessary to develop a better understanding of the forces that shape total factor productivity.

Technological change is an important determinant of TFP. This was Solow's original view, as well as the view of both his disciples and his critics. And Simon Kuznets, who produced landmark studies of the wealth of nations, was quite explicit about his own conviction concerning the preeminence of technology: "we may say that certainly since the second half of the nineteenth century, the major source of economic growth in the developed countries has been science-based technology—in the electrical, internal combustion, electronic, nuclear, and biological fields, among others" (1966, 10). Numerous economic historians have also placed the evolution of technology at the center of modern economic growth. Prominent among them are Landes (1969), Rosenberg (1982), and Mokyr (1990). Their detailed studies of technological change suggest that not only has technological change been indispensable in the formation of the modern industrial sector, but the process by which technology has shaped economic activity has played out over long periods of time. Prominent examples of the development and diffusion of major technologies that spanned many decades include the steam engine, which provided a reliable source of energy, and the dynamo, which enabled flexible manufacturing through the use of electricity in manufacturing plants. Economic historians have urged economists to take a long-term view of the growth process, because the impact of new technologies takes a long time to diffuse.

Despite ups and downs, the average growth rate of the world economy has accelerated over time (see Figure 1.5). This long-run trend cannot be explained by the forces of accumulation that are the cornerstone of Solow's model, because his model predicts declining growth rates. To reconcile the evidence on the acceleration in the rate of growth with the evidence on accumulation, technological change has to be rising over time, and rising fast enough to overcome the curtailing effects of accumulation. This line of reasoning raises the natural question, Why has the pace of technological change been rising over time? To answer this question, we need a theory that explains technological change.

## First Wave

Solow's 1956 study engendered a stream of research during the sixties, which extended and elaborated his basic approach. But this effort came to a halt in the early seventies. And despite some notable exceptions—such as Arrow's (1962a) model of learning by doing, Uzawa's (1965) model of human-capital-driven productivity improvements, and Shell's (1967) model of inventive activity—growth theory remained predominantly a theory of exogenous technological change. As macroeconomists plunged into debates about rational expectations and the effectiveness of monetary policy, interest in growth economics faded away. New Keynesian and New Classical approaches to business cycles occupied center stage, while the study of growth remained on the sidelines.

But then the interest in growth theory abruptly revived. After years of neglect, it resurfaced with a vengeance in the 1980s. The two key papers were by Romer (1986) and Lucas (1988).

Romer noted that historical data do not display declining growth rates. First, the evidence about the world's economic leaders—the Netherlands in the eighteenth century, the UK in the nineteenth century, and the United States in the twentieth century—portrays rising rather than declining growth rates of income per man-hour. That is, the UK grew faster than the Netherlands and the United States grew faster than the UK.[1] Second, using Maddison's (1979) data on growth rates of GDP per capita, Romer calculated decade-long average annual growth rates for eleven countries. For every country he then estimated the probability that in two randomly drawn decades, the rate of growth of the later decade would be higher. The results are depicted in Figure 4.1. The probabilities exceed one-half for each of

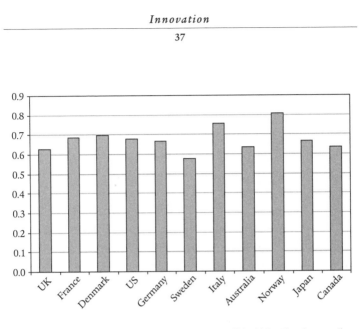

**Figure 4.1** Probability that growth in a later decade will be higher than in an earlier decade, 1700–1978. Data from Romer (1986).

the countries, implying that a country was more likely to experience a rising growth rate than a declining one. Third, he showed that the rate of growth of the U.S. economy has been rising since 1800.[2]

This evidence led Romer to conclude that a Solow-type model with a constant exogenous rate of technological change is inadequate for explaining long-run economic trends. Instead, he proposed a model that emphasizes externalities in the accumulation of knowledge. In this view, output depends on conventional inputs, such as labor and capital, but it also depends on an economy's stock of knowledge. The stock of knowledge rises over time, as business firms invest in knowledge accumulation. Every firm has a production function in which output depends on the firm's private inputs, including the firm's stock of private knowledge, and it also depends on the economy's aggregate public stock of knowledge. Therefore each firm has an incentive to invest in private knowledge. Inadvertently, however, this investment contributes to the aggregate public stock of knowledge. Hence the externality.

What motivated Romer to resort to externalities? In the presence of externalities there can be aggregate increasing returns to scale, and yet every firm can be a price taker, because it perceives a declining marginal productivity of the inputs under its direct control. As a result, the specification of externalities provides a convenient way for handling economies of scale without the need to introduce a noncompetitive market structure. One can view this specification as a dynamic extension of the static version of external economies that was originally developed by Marshall (1920). A similar extension was used by Arrow (1962a) in his model of learning-by-doing. In Romer's framework the externality resides in knowledge; in Arrow's framework it resides in capital.

A firm that accumulates private knowledge inadvertently contributes to the aggregate stock of public knowledge, and the stock of public knowledge raises everyone's productivity. Under these circumstances the declining marginal productivity of private knowledge permits all firms to behave competitively, that is, to be price takers, while the economy encounters economies of scale with rising marginal productivity of knowledge. Importantly, without diminishing returns to aggregate knowledge, the growth rate does not have to decline; it can rise over time until it converges on a constant growth rate in the long run, or it can rise without bound.[3] A model of this type is consistent with a variety of growth patterns, including the patterns displayed by the data.

Lucas (1988) also resorted to externalities. Unlike Romer (1986), however, he introduced them in human capital. In one version of his approach, aggregate output was assumed to depend on physical capital (that is, machines, equipment, and structures), on aggregate human capital (measured as aggregate skills), and on the average level of human capital of the workforce. Physical capital and aggregate human capital were subjected to diminishing returns, but their combined effect on output was assumed to be larger the higher the average level of human capital in the economy. Consequently, the externality resided in the effect of average human capital on output.

Individuals were assumed to devote effort to the accumulation of human capital. The rise in the individual stock of human capital was a function of this effort and the level of human capital already attained. Using Uzawa's (1965) specification of this relationship, in which the rate of accumulation is proportional to the stock of human capital, Lucas showed that such an economy grows in the long run at a rate that exceeds the rate of technological progress. Its growth rate depends on features of its technology for producing goods and services and on features of its "technology" for producing human capital.

In another version of human capital externalities, Lucas considered specialized human capital. A sector's output level was assumed to be proportional to the sector-specific stock of human capital and to the workforce employed by the sector. Unlike the pervious model, however, in this version the sector-specific human capital stock was assumed to grow as a result of sector-specific learning-by-doing. The increase in the stock of human capital was assumed to be proportional to the product of the sector's stock of human capital and the fraction of the workforce employed by the sector. Under these circumstances the economy grows in the long run even without technological change, because learning-by-doing becomes an engine of growth. When goods are highly substitutable for each other, the sector with the fastest rate of learning grows in importance over time, until it takes over the entire economy. And when goods are poor substitutes for each other, the economy converges to a long-run equilibrium with a balanced sectoral structure, in which the rate of growth of human capital is the same in every sector.

Models of human capital accumulation require careful interpretation. More often than not, empirical researchers use measures of human capital that are based on years of schooling. In this event, human capital per person cannot grow without bound, because individual lifetimes are finite. As a result, the growth of human capital cannot be a source of permanent economic expansion. In contrast, many theoretical models, such as Lucas's (1988) model, view human capital as a measure of skills that can expand without bound. Under these circumstances human capital accumulation can serve as a source of permanent long-run growth. It is clear that alternative treatments of human capital have dramatically different implications. One major issue that arises in this context is whether human capital is embodied in human beings only or also in the society. After all, if human capital is not embodied only in individuals, how different is it from Romer's "stock of knowledge"? My sense is that both the conceptual and the operational meanings of this distinction have not yet been sufficiently clarified.

Education is an important mechanism for human capital formation, and productivity-weighted years of schooling provide a natural yardstick for measuring the stock of human capital. As already noted, however, the accumulation of this type of human capital cannot feed long-run growth. Despite this limitation, researchers have found repeatedly that education plays a major role in economic growth. Using growth accounting, Goldin and Katz (2001) found that during the twentieth century about a quarter of the U.S. growth in income per worker was due to the rise in education.[4] And Mitch (2001) found that while the spread of primary education in Europe in the late nineteenth century made only a modest contribution to European economic growth, the spread of secondary and tertiary education in the twentieth century had a large impact, though not as large in Europe as in the United States. Finally, Young (1995) found that the rise in years of schooling played a central role in the growth of the Asian NICs. Similar results have been obtained for many other countries and for different periods of time. Education plays an important role in accounting for the time pattern of economic growth and the cross-country variation in income per capita.[5]

The remaining question to examine is whether there are human capital externalities, because such externalities are required for human-capital-driven sustained long-run growth. On this point the evidence is mixed. On the one hand, Acemoglu and Angrist (2001) did not find such externalities in micro data, and Cohen and Soto (2001) did not find such externalities in macro data. In particular, Cohen and Soto found that the rate of return on investment in education, estimated from macro data, is comparable in size to the rates of return that have been estimated from micro data sets with wage equations. On the other hand, Moretti (2002) found positive externalities from college graduates on wages of other workers. Specifically, he found that wages of otherwise similar workers are higher in U.S. cities with larger shares of college graduates in the labor force. This implies that the social rate of return on higher education is higher than the private rate of return.

I view these findings—namely, that economists have not been able so far to turn out decisive evidence in favor of human capital externalities—as tentative only. My strong prior assumption is that workers do learn from each other, and therefore one should expect a worker to be more productive in an environment with more-educated coworkers. There are many difficulties in estimating externalities generally and human capital externalities in particular, and Krueger and Lindahl (2001) discuss some of the problems involved. For these reasons the current evidence is unlikely to be definitive.

Are there externalities in the accumulation of knowledge? Arrow (1962b) comprehensively analyzed the allocation of resources to inventive activities, and answered affirmatively. Romer (1986) expanded this discussion, arguing forcefully that not only do such externalities exist, but they are a major feature of modern economies and a source of economic growth. The key argument advanced by Arrow was that information, unlike ordinary goods, can be repeatedly used by individuals and business firms without being depleted, and that individuals and business firms cannot be excluded from the use of information that becomes public. For this reason the benefits of new knowledge are not limited to its original creators: hence the externality.[6]

Research and development (R&D) creates new knowledge. As a result, if knowledge externalities do exist, they should show up in R&D activities. And indeed many empirical studies point to the existence of externalities in R&D. Griliches (1979) reported high rates of return on R&D investment for the postwar period. First, *private* rates of return were high. In the United States, which has been studied in some detail, these rates were more than twice as high as the rates of return on investment in physical capital. In other countries this ratio was even higher.[7] Although part of this gap may reflect the required compensation for higher risk, it is unlikely that the entire gap was due to this compensation. Second, estimated rates of return doubled when account was taken of spillovers across firms in the same sector, and they rose further when account was taken of the spread of benefits from sectors that invested in R&D to technologically related sectors.[8] It seems evident that the social rate of return to R&D investment is much higher than the private rate of return, a clear indication of externalities. This evidence justifies the second wave of "new" growth theory, which has emphasized innovation as a proximate source of productivity growth.

## Second Wave

Romer (1990) also initiated the second wave of research on the "new" growth theory. Instead of the aggregate approach to knowledge accumulation that he had pursued in 1986, in 1990 he developed a disaggregated model of the business sector in order to study the evolution of productivity. In this model, business firms invest resources in R&D in order to develop new products. The blueprints for these products are protected by patents. As a result, innovators gain monopoly power which they can use to beef up profits, and the additional profits provide incentives for investment in R&D. As with many other types of investment opportunities, innovators make investment decisions on the basis of a comparison of the present value of future profits from their investment with the upfront R&D costs. Competition attracts entrants into the invention activity up to the point at which the private rate of return to R&D is equalized with the rate of return on alternative investment projects.

The private return to R&D depends on institutional features, such as the length of patent protection, the coverage of trademark protection, the efficacy with which the legal system protects intellectual property rights, and the nature of the regulatory framework within which business firms operate. Be this as it may, no system provides full protection. As a result, some useful knowledge that is generated in the course of inventive activities within one firm becomes available to others.

Romer formalized a mechanism that captures these effects. A major novelty was his modeling of the relationship between the productivity of resources in R&D and the cumulative investment in it. In the model, innovators aim to invent new products, which provide them with profits and thereby an incentive to innovate. But inadvertently, they also create knowledge that is not embodied in blueprints and cannot be retained as a trade secret. This "disembodied" knowledge becomes available to other innovators and thereby reduces future R&D costs for everyone. Under these circumstances, the stock of knowledge available to innovators is a function of past R&D efforts. The more R&D was performed in the past the larger this stock and the cheaper it is to do R&D today.

This mechanism—of forward R&D spillovers—reduces R&D costs over time. But as more and more products are invented, competition among their suppliers cuts into the profits of each of them, leading to declining profits per product. It follows that the incentive to innovate rises or declines over time, depending on how fast the costs of R&D fall relative to profits. Romer identified technological features that lead to the balancing of these forces, so that the incentive to innovate remains constant over time and, as a result, the resources deployed to R&D activities remain constant as well. An economy that follows this type of trajectory experiences a constant rate of productivity growth. And this rate is endogenous in the sense that it depends on the economy's characteristics, especially features that determine the rate of saving. Economies with higher savings rates grow faster because they allocate (endogenously) more resources to inventive activities. Unlike Solow's model, Romer's model predicts a link between resource allocation and productivity growth.[9]

A company that takes out a patent on an invention often thereby discloses important information about its technology. This information becomes public once the patent has been registered. Using patent citation data, Jaffe and Trajtenberg (2002) have shown convincingly that this is an important channel of technological diffusion. Unlike the studies that have identified a gap between the social and private rates of return to R&D, which provide evidence in favor of R&D spillovers but do not identify a specific mechanism for their transmission, Jaffe and Trajtenberg have identified an important mechanism that supports Romer's model.[10]

Romer (1990) analyzed an economy in which all products are equally substitutable for each other and the available assortment of products expands through innovation. Alternative analytical frameworks were developed by Grossman and Helpman (1991a,b) and Aghion and Howitt (1992). In these models products improve along quality ladders. Every new product is highly substitutable for a similar product of lower quality, but less substitutable for other products. As in Romer's model, however, there are forward spillovers from current innovators to future innovators, because the existing quality provides a benchmark from which innovators attempt to further improve the product.

The resulting growth process is one of "creative destruction," as higher-quality products destroy market opportunities for older, lower-quality products.[11] Productivity grows over time as a result of quality improvements. The rate of improvement varies across sectors, because the sectoral improvement rates follow a random process. Nevertheless, when an economy has many sectors, the average rate of improvement is not stochastic, and this average rate can be described by a well-defined function of the economy's characteristics. For some versions of this model the reduced-form equations—which describe the links between an economy's features and its rate of growth—are almost identical to a version of Romer's model, despite the differences in approach. For this reason Romer's model of expanding product variety exhibits similar dynamics to the expanding quality models of Grossman and Helpman and of Aghion and Howitt.[12]

## R&D Levels

Figure 4.2 presents data on investment in nondefense R&D as a fraction of GDP in the seven largest economies (G7). The important point to note is that there are wide variations in these ratios. While Italy invested around 1 percent of its income during the eighteen-year period from 1981 to 1998, Japan invested more than 2 percent, and in 1998 the investment rate in Japan was three times as high as in Italy. These data exhibit variation across countries and variation over time. In larger samples of countries, the variation was even greater. Sweden, for example, invested more than Japan while Greece invested less than Italy.

Another point to note is that investment in R&D is substantially smaller than investment in physical capital, which is often five to ten times larger. Does this imply that investment in R&D

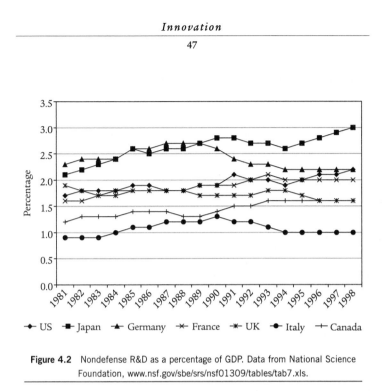

**Figure 4.2** Nondefense R&D as a percentage of GDP. Data from National Science Foundation, www.nsf.gov/sbe/srs/nsf01309/tables/tab7.xls.

is necessarily less important? No, for two reasons: first, because the rate of return on R&D is many times higher than the rate of return on investment in machines and equipment; and second, because whenever R&D raises total factor productivity, the higher TFP level induces capital accumulation. As a result, R&D has both a direct and an indirect effect on output, and the indirect effect can be large. I will discuss the quantitative nature of this decomposition in the next chapter. At this point it suffices to note that the model of quality ladders can be calibrated to fit the U.S. data reasonable well (see Grossman and Helpman 1994a, 35).

A more detailed study of the U.S. economy is provided by Jones (2002).[13] He found that between 1950 and 1993 improvements in educational attainments, which amounted to an increase of four years of schooling on average, explain about 30 percent of the growth in output per hour. The remaining 70 percent is attributable to the rise in the stock of ideas that was produced in the United States, France, West Germany, the United Kingdom, and Japan. Reviewing the evidence on the effects of R&D on total factor productivity, Mohnen (1996, 56) reported that one study attributed between 10 percent and 50 percent of output growth in the major OECD countries to R&D growth, a second study attributed 40 percent of U.S. TFP growth to R&D spillovers, and a third study attributed 66 percent of TFP growth in Japan to U.S. R&D growth.

## Scale Effects

The first-generation models of innovation-driven growth were criticized for their scale effects. In their simplest version, with one input called labor, they predict that larger countries—that is, countries with a larger labor force—will grow faster. The evidence for the post–World War II period does not support this prediction.[14] Moreover, as Jones (1995a) argued, even when one examines the time pattern of the resources allocated to R&D and the trend in total factor productivity, the relationship between these two time series is not consistent with the models developed by Romer (1990), Grossman and Helpman (1991a,b), and Aghion and Howitt (1992). While the number of scientists and engineers engaged in R&D was rising in France, Germany, Japan, and the United States at a rapid rate over several decades, TFP growth did not exhibit a comparable upward trend. If anything, TFP growth slowed in many countries after the oil crisis of 1973.[15]

In response, the models were altered in various ways in order to dampen the effect of scale on the rate of productivity growth.[16] Jones (1995b) and Segerstrom (1998) introduced crowding into the R&D activity, and thereby eliminated the long-run effect of size on productivity growth. Young (1998) combined the expanding-variety features from Romer's (1990) paper with the rising-quality features from the Grossman and Helpman (1991a) and Aghion and Howitt (1992) papers into a unified model without the effects of scale on long-run productivity growth. In Young's model long-run productivity growth is driven by growth in product quality. But a larger economy produces more varieties, which requires spreading the quality-improving R&D effort over a wider range of products. As a result, the additional resources that a larger economy attracts to product-improvement activities are just sufficient to compensate for the spread of these resources over more products, so that in the end the average pace of improvement remains the same. To be sure, there is a scale effect in this model, in the sense that income per capita is higher in larger economies. But the growth rate of income per capita is not.[17]

These modifications eliminated the influence of economic policies on long-run growth that existed in the first-generation models. As Young explained:

> One can easily see how many policy interventions, which in contemporary models of endogenous innovation influence the long-run growth of the economy, will be ineffective (in growth rates) in this model. Thus the imposition of tariffs, on either a unilateral or multilateral basis, or the provision of proportional R&D subsidies (which rebate a fixed share of R&D expenditures) will change the total pool of rents available to entrepreneurs without in-

fluencing the elasticity of demand with respect to product quality. These policies will influence the level of income, without changing its long-run growth rate. (1998, 52–53)

In response, Howitt (1999) modified Young's model in a way that allowed population growth to feed into the growth process. His model gives rise to a long-run rate of productivity growth that is higher in economies with faster population growth. Moreover, unlike Young's model, his model predicts a positive effect of R&D subsidies on long-run growth and a positive effect of savings.[18]

Alternative ways of circumscribing the effects of scale on the longrun rate of growth have different implications for the long-run time trend of the resources employed in R&D: the Jones (1995b) model implies a constant real value of these resources, while the Howitt (1999) model implies a growth rate of their real value that equals the rate of real GDP growth. The evidence reported in Aghion and Howitt (forthcoming) does not reject the stationarity of the U.S. time series of the fraction of GDP spent on innovative activities, which is consistent with Howitt's model, but it rejects the stationarity of the time series of real resources employed in R&D, which is not consistent with Jones's model.

All these developments notwithstanding, it is important to note the inherent link in this theory between market size and the incentive to innovate. Since the incentive to innovate is larger the more plentiful are the monopoly profits from new products—be they horizontally or vertically differentiated—and since the monopoly profits from new products are higher the larger the market in which the products are sold, it follows that larger markets encourage more R&D. There seems to be an inherent scale effect in this view of the world. One can magnify the strength of this scale effect or one can dampen it, but one cannot eliminate it.[19]

## General Purpose Technologies

My discussion of technological progress has been confined so far to studies that view it as an incremental process. This has been the prevalent approach in the literature. Economic historians, such as Landes (1969) and Rosenberg (1982), have even argued that small improvements have been the predominant form of technological change. There are exceptions, however. Best known among them are the steam engine, electricity, and the computer. Each one of these inventions was drastic rather than incremental; each had the potential for pervasive use in a wide range of applications, each triggered the development of many complementary inputs, and each launched a prolonged process of adjustment that included the reorganization of the workplace.[20] Bresnahan and Trajtenberg (1995) coined the term "general purpose technologies" (GPTs) to describe technologies of this type.[21]

Growth that is driven by general purpose technologies is different from growth driven by incremental innovations. Unlike incremental innovations, GPTs can trigger an uneven growth trajectory, which starts with a prolonged slowdown followed by a fast acceleration. Different arguments have been offered to explain such cycles. First, Hornstein and Krusell (1996) and Greenwood and Yorokolgu (1997) argued that the adoption of new technologies requires firms to learn how to use them, and this learning process slows down productivity growth. Second, Helpman and Trajtenberg (1998) suggested instead that it takes time

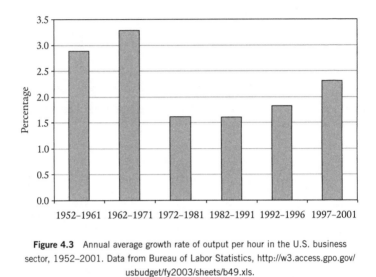

**Figure 4.3** Annual average growth rate of output per hour in the U.S. business sector, 1952–2001. Data from Bureau of Labor Statistics, http://w3.access.gpo.gov/usbudget/fy2003/sheets/b49.xls.

to develop complementary inputs that can be used with new technologies, and that during the phase in which resources are diverted to the development of these inputs, growth slows down. Third, Helpman and Rangel (1999) argued that on-the-job training, which raises the productivity of workers, can be the source of a slowdown. If experience is technology specific, then workers who switch to a new technology lose some of their skills. They may choose to switch nevertheless if they expect wages to grow quickly as they accumulate experience with the new technology. Under these circumstances growth may temporarily decline as a result of the decline in labor productivity. All these arguments have been used to explain the decline in productivity growth in the post–oil crisis period, treating the introduction of comput-

**Figure 4.4** U.S. market capitalization relative to GDP. Data from Greenwood and Jovanovic (1999) and Federal Reserve Board of Governors.

ing technology—or the microprocessor—as the arrival of a new GPT.

This sharp decline in the growth rate of output per hour in the U.S. business sector is depicted in Figure 4.3. From an average growth rate of more than 3 percent in the 1960s, the growth rate declined to half this value in the 1970s and 1980s. And only in the 1990s did the growth rate of output per hour accelerate.

Helpman and Trajtenberg (1998) also showed that a new GPT can produce a cycle in the value of the stock market relative to GDP. The arrival of a new GPT reduces the value of firms that use the old technology. In the meantime the new technology is not very productive, because it takes time to develop its complementary inputs and organizational forms. As a result, the value of the stock market falls relative to GDP. The stock market is depressed despite the entry of firms based on the new GPT, because their aggregate value is low initially. But as they become a larger part of the economy, they exert a more pronounced effect on the stock market. As a result, the stock market starts to rise faster than GDP.

This type of evolution of the U.S. stock market was documented by Greenwood and Jovanovic (1999). As Figure 4.4 shows, there was a marked decline in the stock market relative to GDP in the early seventies, from a ratio of one to about one-half.[22] The ratio started to rise in the late eighties, surpassing the previous peak in the mid-nineties.[23] The figure describes a long cycle that is consistent with GPT-driven growth.

# 5

## INTERDEPENDENCE

We have seen that countries grow as a result of physical and human capital accumulation, and by improvements in total factor productivity. Productivity has played a particularly large role in modern economic growth. It accounts for more than half the variation across countries in income per capita, and much more than half the variation across countries in growth rates of income per capita. Therefore, to understand the sources of economic growth, one must understand what causes productivity growth. But a satisfactory understanding of economic growth also requires an appreciation of how countries interact with each other, because countries' income levels are interdependent. In some instances this interdependence is direct, in others indirect, via productivity.

As a case in point, note that the high rate of growth of the world economy between 1870 and 1913 occurred in a period of rapid expansion of international trade, as did the rapid growth of the world economy in the post–World War II era. These trends are evident from a comparison of Figures 1.5 and 5.1.[1] O'Rourke

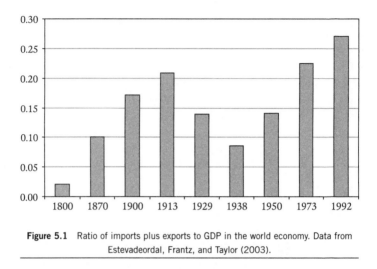

**Figure 5.1** Ratio of imports plus exports to GDP in the world economy. Data from Estevadeordal, Frantz, and Taylor (2003).

and Williamson (1999) describe the years 1870–1913 as the first wave of globalization, characterized by an unprecedented expansion of international trade, investment, and migration. The second wave of globalization occurred in the post–World War II era, driven initially by trade and subsequently by trade and investment. Also apparent from these figures is the fact that during the years between the two world wars—in which there was a major retraction from a liberal trading order—trade declined and so did growth. According to Figure 5.1, trade was 2 percent of GDP in 1800 and increased to almost 21 percent in 1913, at the dawn of World War I. After the war the trade ratio declined. It started to rise again only after World War II, reaching the 1913 peak in the early 1970s.

Are these developments in trade and growth coincidental? Or is there an underlying relationship between the degree of international integration and the growth of income per capita? The main theme of this chapter is that international integration has sizable effects on economic growth. Integration unleashes forces of convergence on the one hand and forces of divergence on the other. What these forces are and how they operate is elucidated below.

## Terms of Trade

Capital accumulation raises income per capita. As the capital-labor ratio rises, however, the increasing capital stock contributes to output at a diminishing rate and the incentive to accumulate declines. Growth is thus limited by the degree of diminishing returns, as we saw in Chapter 2.

This argument takes a different form in an open economy that engages in international trade, because trade permits a country to specialize and specialization affects the return to capital. Small countries in particular can avoid the curse of diminishing returns, because their terms of trade are not sensitive to the size of their capital stock.[2]

Consider, for example, a small country whose terms of trade are fixed; that is, world prices of its exportables and importables are constant, no matter whether the country grows or not. If this country were to specialize in one product only, say garments, then its accumulation of capital would raise the output of garments, which the country would be able to exchange at fixed prices for all other goods in the world's markets. But because of diminishing returns, every additional unit of capital would produce a declining increment in revenue from the sales of garments, and therefore a declining purchasing power on world markets.

Now suppose that this country can also produce toys, which are more capital intensive than garments. When the country has a low capital-to-labor ratio it specializes in the production of garments, despite the fact that it knows how to produce toys. This is efficient. In the initial phase of capital accumulation the country may remain specialized in garments. But at some point, when its capital-labor ratio becomes high enough, the country finds it profitable to also produce toys. As a result, some of its resources move into the toy industry. Further increases in the capital-labor ratio lead to further shifts of resources from garments to toys, but as long as it pays to produce both products, this reallocation does not affect the marginal productivity of capital. It follows that the country escapes the curse of diminishing returns as long as its production is diversified between garments and toys, and therefore the depressing effect of capital accumulation on the growth rate of income per capita is mitigated in these circumstances. International trade theory predicts that the country will produce both garments and toys if and only if its capital-labor ratio is between the capital-labor ratios used in these industries.

The argument generalizes to many sectors that differ in capital intensity; there are then many regions of diversification. In economies of this type capital accumulation leads to shifts in specialization toward sectors with ever higher capital intensity, but the marginal productivity of capital declines only during the transition from one region of diversification to the next.[3]

Ventura (1997) argued that this explains why small countries can grow fast—because they can escape the adverse effects of diminishing returns. Such countries follow a development path on which the sectoral composition of output shifts over time, toward products that are more capital intensive or more human-capital intensive. This prediction fits the Asian NICs particularly well. Young (1992) documented a transformation of this type in Hong Kong and Singapore.

Large countries are prone to the curse of diminishing returns, however, because whenever a large country expands the supply of one of its products it thereby depresses the product's price on world markets. As a result, the value of the output declines, magnifying the effect of diminishing returns to accumulation. The importance of this effect was studied by Acemoglu and Ventura (2002), who pointed out that growth that affects the terms of trade adversely leads to convergence, just as diminishing returns do. They also found evidence for a negative cross-country correlation between the growth of income per capita and the growth of the terms of trade. Between 1965 and 1985 a 1 percent faster growth rate accelerated the deterioration of the terms of trade by approximately 0.6 percent.

Terms-of-trade movements provide an important mechanism for the international transmission of growth effects. If, as Acemoglu and Ventura argued, growing countries suffer from deteriorating terms of trade, then their trading partners enjoy improving terms of trade. As a result, a growing country confers benefits on its trade partners. In other words, the benefits of growth are diffused throughout the world via terms-of-trade adjustments.[4]

The work of Acemoglu and Ventura notwithstanding, trade theory suggests that the effects of accumulation on the terms of trade vary with the characteristics of the growing country. Moreover, these effects depend on what drives foreign trade. For example, the factor proportions theory of international trade does not predict an unconditional negative relationship between a country's capital stock and its terms of trade. According to this theory, a larger capital stock deteriorates the terms of trade of a country that exports capital-intensive products but improves the terms of trade of a country that exports labor-intensive products. For this reason the 0.6 percent coefficient that was estimated by Acemoglu and Ventura represents a cross-country average effect at best, and it may not apply to any country in particular.

## Diffusion of Knowledge

Important as terms of trade may be, they provide but one channel of transmission of economic developments. Knowledge flows breed additional interdependencies across countries. In this and the next section I discuss how knowledge flows link income levels and growth rates. Inadvertent accumulation of knowledge via learning-by-doing is examined in this section; the ramifications of investment in R&D are explored in the next.

Learning-by-doing has a long tradition in international trade. It is typically formulated as a positive effect of cumulative output on an industry's total factor productivity. That is, the larger an industry's past cumulative output level, the higher its stock of knowledge and the more productive its inputs.[5] In a world that consists of a single country, the scope for this type of Marshallian economy of scale is naturally limited to that country's industry. But in a world of many countries additional possibilities arise. Learning-by-doing in, say, the German chemical industry may be limited to the cumulative experience of the German chemical industry, or it may depend on the cumulative experience of the Swiss chemical industry as well. More generally, it may depend on the cumulative experience of the world's chemical industry. What is the correct formulation? And does it matter?

The first point to note is that it matters a lot. The extent of international spillovers of learning-by-doing affects both the structure of foreign trade and the growth rates of countries. And while this type of learning may be country specific in some sectors, it may be international in scope in others.[6]

To see how learning-by-doing affects specialization, trade, and growth, imagine a country that produces two products, with learning-by-doing taking place in each of them. The available resources cannot be expanded, implying that productivity is the only viable source of growth. Also suppose that initially the country does not trade with the outside world. Then total factor productivity rises in every sector at a rate that depends on the sector's output level and the sector-specific speed of learning. A sector with faster learning experiences faster growth of its stock of knowledge and faster TFP growth.

Grossman and Helpman (1995) pointed out that under these circumstances, a country's aggregate productivity growth depends in the long run on its demand structure and on its initial stocks of knowledge. In particular, if the two goods are highly substitutable for each other in the eyes of the consumers, then in the long run the country is led to specialize in the production of one product only. Which product it is depends on the initial conditions. Namely, it depends on the relative sectoral stocks of knowledge. When this relative stock crosses a threshold in favor of one particular sector, the favored sector expands at a faster rate, dominating the economy in the long run. The lower the speed of learning in the favored sector and the lower its intrinsic productivity level in comparison with the other sector, the higher the threshold. As a result, the long-run rate of growth of income per capita is higher the larger the economy, the faster the learning-by-doing in the favored sector, and the higher the intrinsic productivity level of the favored sector.

Note that in this economy the long-run rate of growth depends on initial conditions; it can be higher or lower depending on which sector is favored by the initial relative stock of knowledge. An economy whose initial conditions favor the sector with the slow growth potential grows slowly in the long run, while an economy whose initial conditions favor the sector with the high growth potential grows quickly in the long run. Evidently market forces do not necessarily secure the fastest growth trajectory. This is very different from the neoclassical growth model, in which growth is driven by factor accumulation and the long-run growth rate does not depend on initial conditions.

Next suppose that there are two economies of this type, each one in specialized equilibrium with a constant rate of growth. They differ in learning speeds, in intrinsic productivity levels, and in size. Also suppose that these countries decide to trade with each other. How will trade affect their growth rates? The answer to this question depends decisively on whether trade opens up the possibility of cross-border learning-by-doing.

First, consider the case in which learning-by-doing becomes international in scope and, in particular, suppose that knowledge spills over to foreign firms as fast as it does across domestic firms. And moreover, suppose that knowledge becomes immediately available to all of them. Under these circumstances both countries have the same stocks of knowledge and their initial patterns of specialization in the trading era are determined by comparative advantage, that is, by their intrinsic relative productivity levels. The growth rate of an industry's stock of knowledge is then determined by the intrinsic productivity level of the country that specializes in this industry and by the industry's speed of learning and size. Grossman and Helpman (1995) show that this pattern of interdependence can produce a variety of outcomes. Trade may drive a country to specialize in a sector with low growth potential, slowing down its long-run growth relative to autarky. Or it can drive a country to specialize in a sector with high growth potential, thereby accelerating its long-run growth. But it is also possible that both countries will grow faster in the long run. The outcome depends on the size of the countries, their intrinsic productivity levels, and their speeds of learning.[7]

Second, consider the case in which learning-by-doing is national in scope. In this case the initial post-autarky patterns of specialization become entrenched, because every country becomes more productive in the sectors in which it has a comparative advantage and its comparative advantage only strengthens over time. Krugman (1987) gave the clearest account of the resulting paths of development of economies of this type in a world with two countries, many products, and unitary elasticities of substitution in demand. The growth rates of income per capita do not converge under these circumstances. That is, international trade does not lead to convergence.[8]

Two important points emerge from these examples. First, international trade does not necessarily lead to the convergence of growth rates. Second, even when it does, it does not necessarily lead to faster growth for all countries. Although trade unleashes forces of convergence, it also unleashes forces of divergence. Which of the two dominates depends in subtle ways on various economic features that interact with one another.[9]

Additional insights about these issues arise from an examination of the purposeful accumulation of knowledge via investment in research and development. Unlike inadvertent learning-by-doing, R&D responds to economic incentives.[10] As a result, the economic environment directly affects the level of this activity, which in turn affects productivity growth.

## Research and Development

We saw in the previous chapter the ways in which investment in R&D affects economic growth. I argued that the "new" growth theory emphasized two main channels of influence: one through the impact on the range of available products, the other through the impact on the stock of knowledge available for research and development. There, however, the discussion was confined to closed economies. It is now time to examine how international trade interacts with these channels of influence. An understanding of these interactions is particularly important because more than 95 percent of the world's R&D is performed by the industrial countries. If the benefits of innovation are confined to the countries that invest in R&D, then research and development could produce major disparities in living standards. Kuznets, for one, was mindful of the international repercussions of R&D activities. He wrote: "No matter where these technological and social innovations emerge—and they are largely the product of the developed countries—the economic growth of any given nation depends upon their adoption . . . Given this worldwide validity and the transmissibility of modern additions to knowledge, the transnational character of this stock of knowledge and the dependence on it of any single nation in the course of its modern economic growth become apparent" (Kuznets 1966, 287).

The modern literature on trade and growth has identified a

number of channels through which R&D links the productivity levels of various countries. Grossman and Helpman (1991b) discuss these channels in great detail. First, there is the market-size effect. Having access to a larger market raises the profitability of inventive activities and encourages investment in R&D. In a closed economy this effect favors larger countries. In open economies trade affords access to world markets to both small and large countries. As a result, trade boosts investment in R&D and the growth of productivity, and it does so more in smaller countries.

Second, there is a competition effect. Integration into a trading system exposes domestic firms to foreign competition. If this competition hurts profits, investment in innovative activities declines, because lower profits provide a lower stimulus to R&D. The negative effect of competition on R&D has been emphasized by most of the literature. Competition can also raise the incentive to innovate, however, by inducing technological leaders to forge ahead more quickly in order to avoid competition from technological followers. In this case trade boosts R&D.[11]

Third, trade and foreign direct investment (FDI) change domestic factor prices. If the resulting shift makes R&D cheaper, investment in inventive activities rises. Otherwise it declines. Grossman and Helpman (1991b, chap. 6) provided a telling example. They considered a small country that produces two products whose prices are set by world markets. Every sector uses a primary input and an assortment of differentiated intermediate inputs. The intermediate inputs are not traded internationally, and they are developed by domestic firms with the aid of an R&D technology. The R&D technology is intensive in human capital, as is one of the final-good sectors. Grossman and Helpman showed that opening to trade accelerates this economy's rate of TFP growth if and only if the relative price of the product that is human-capital intensive is lower on world markets than in the economy under autarky.[12] This illustrates a mechanism through which trade may promote or hinder R&D-driven productivity growth. In this example there are no international R&D spillovers, so that domestic firms learn only from other domestic firms, but not from foreign firms. And similarly, foreign firms do not learn from domestic firms.

This example also shows that protection may accelerate or slow down growth. In an economy that imports the product that is human-capital intensive, protection raises the price of this product and the cost of R&D. As a result, investment in R&D declines and growth slows down. But in an economy that exports the human-capital-intensive product, protection reduces the relative price of this good and reduces the cost of R&D. As a result, investment in R&D expands and growth speeds up. So the theory does not predict a negative relationship between protection and growth for all countries. The effect of protection on growth depends on a country's characteristics.

Fourth, trade eliminates redundancy in R&D races. When countries are isolated from one another, a firm operating in one country attempts to develop products that are not produced by other firms in this country only. Such a firm has no incentive to differentiate its product from goods that are produced in foreign countries, because it does not expect to compete with foreign suppliers in the domestic market. As a result, duplication of R&D efforts may exist. When countries trade with each other, however, every firm competes with all other suppliers worldwide. Under these circumstances a firm has an incentive to differentiate its product from all the other products in the world economy. This minimizes the duplication of R&D efforts and therefore brings about faster growth of R&D stocks of knowledge and lower R&D costs. The outcome is faster productivity growth.

Fifth, access to foreign suppliers provides access to specialized intermediate inputs and capital goods that are produced in other countries. In addition to the standard gains from trade that are price related, this type of trade generates additional gains by expanding the assortment of inputs available for production. The larger assortment of inputs raises TFP.[13]

Finally, in a world of many countries, the stock of knowledge that affects R&D costs can be shared by all countries or it can be country specific. That is, a country's R&D—which raises its stock of useful knowledge for future inventive activities—may or may not contribute to the stocks of knowledge available to other countries. This distinction is similar to the one made in the previous section between country-specific and worldwide stocks of knowledge that are created by learning-by-doing. When these R&D spillovers are international in scope, they activate convergence forces. And when they are country specific, they activate divergence forces.

The power of these convergence forces was illustrated by Grossman and Helpman (1991b, chap. 7).[14] They showed that whenever R&D stocks of knowledge are fully shared by the trading countries, the long-run patterns of trade and growth are independent of initial conditions. Long-run trade patterns are determined by differences in factor proportions, just as in static trade models, and the trading countries share the same rates of TFP growth. That is, productivity growth may differ across sectors, but for a given sector it does not vary across countries. Under these circumstances aggregate TFP growth differs between countries only as a result of differences in the composition of inputs, which produce differences in the composition of outputs.

And when the differences in factor proportions are not large, the real income of an input is the same in every country.[15]

In the absence of international spillovers in R&D stocks of knowledge, divergence is the more likely outcome. Grossman and Helpman (1991b, chap. 8) illustrated this feature with a simple one-factor (labor), two-country model. They showed that in an integrated world economy in which the two countries are of comparable size, the country with the initial advantage in the R&D stock of knowledge widens its advantage over time, because it invests more in R&D. Although this does not always induce differences in factor prices, wages are higher in the country with the initial advantage whenever differences in wages emerge. In this case growth depends on initial conditions. Even minute differences in the initial stocks of knowledge can accumulate over time into huge differences in living standards. And these divergence forces can reduce the growth rate of the initially disadvantaged country.[16]

It is important to note that in this type of environment faster growth is not synonymous with higher welfare. Growth is costly, because it uses up resources that are employed in R&D. For this reason it is not always desirable to move resources into R&D in order to grow faster. At the same time, trade can be welfare improving even when it leads to slower growth, because a country can raise its real income by exchanging goods on world markets. First, a slow-growing country may enjoy terms of trade improvements. Second, when the initial effect of the gains from trade is large enough, it can more than compensate for the slower pace of income expansion. In other words, the static gains may outweigh the dynamic losses.

In sum, the Grossman and Helpman (1991b) theory does not predict a simple relationship between exposure to foreign trade and productivity growth. In theory, trade can encourage or discourage the growth of income per capita.

## Evidence on Trade Volumes

Although in theory trade can promote or hinder growth, there are good reasons to believe that pro-growth forces have dominated the development of many economies. The Italian city-states, such as Genoa and Venice, thrived on trade in the Middle Ages, and they played a key role in fostering the late medieval Commercial Revolution. The Commercial Revolution, in turn, had a considerable impact on European economic development.[17] International trade also interacted in important ways with the Industrial Revolution to promote prosperity in Europe. According to Pomeranz (2000), as recently as the mid-eighteenth century Europe was not more advanced than China. Nevertheless, the two regions followed divergent development paths, with Europe growing much faster in the aftermath of the Industrial Revolution. European trade with the New World made a sizable contribution to this trend.

Galor and Mountford (2003) attribute an especially large role to trade in explaining the Europe-China divergence. They hypothesize that European trade with East Asia drove the East Asian countries to specialize in agriculture, which had low growth potential, and allowed Europe to specialize in manufactures, which had greater growth potential. As a result, Europe forged ahead of East Asia. This hypothesis builds on the arguments for divergence examined in the previous two sections.[18]

Trade also played a central role in the development of Japan. Lockwood (1954) documented the growth of Japanese foreign trade after it opened up to the rest of the world in the second half of the nineteenth century. He pointed out that Japan's growth in the post-Meiji era was enabled to a large extent by its links with the rest of the world, which included trade and the assimilation of foreign technologies.

These historical examples illustrate the direct role that international trade has played in the growth of nations. Another example is the acceleration of growth that followed the Industrial Revolution, which also took place in a period of fast-growing trade (see Figures 1.5 and 5.1). More systematic evidence on cross-country correlations between trade and growth exists, however, for the post–World War II period. Simple estimates of the impact of openness on growth, such as Feder (1982) or Edwards (1992), point to a positive effect.[19] However, more sophisticated estimates—based on the specifications developed by Barro and Sala-i-Martin (1992) and Mankiw, Romer, and Weil (1992) that I discussed in Chapter 3—have yielded mixed results. As Levine and Renelt (1992) pointed out, exports as a fraction of GDP have a positive effect on the growth rate of income per capita when the investment rate is not included as an explanatory variable.[20] But once the investment rate is included, trade exposure has no effect. Yet the investment rate rises with the measure of openness, implying that trade speeds up growth, but only through its effect on investment.

Much of the empirical work on the relationship between trade and growth has been criticized for failing to account for the endogeneity of trade flows and for the fact that exports are part of GDP. The endogeneity of the trade measure produces a simultaneity bias in the estimated impact, while exports—which are part of GDP—are inherently correlated positively with GDP. Frankel and Romer (1999) proposed a methodology for overcoming these shortcomings.

They estimated a gravity equation of bilateral trade flows, in which various geographic characteristics and bilateral distances affect trade.[21] They then used the trade flows predicted by the geographic characteristics and the distances between countries as instruments for trade, in order to estimate the effect of imports plus exports as a fraction of GDP on income per capita. Their equation was similar to the one estimated by Mankiw, Romer, and Weil (1992), except for the addition of the openness measure.

On the basis of the resulting instrumental variables (IV) estimate for the sample of 98 countries used by Mankiw, Romer, and Weil, as well as the estimate for a larger sample of 150 countries, Frankel and Romer found a strong effect of openness on income per capita. Moreover, the resulting impact of the IV estimates was about twice as high as the impact of the ordinary least-squares (OLS) estimates, which suggests that the OLS estimates were not biased upward (see their table 3).[22] According to Frankel and Romer, a 1 percent higher trade share raises income per capita by 2 percent. Decomposing the effects of trade on income into their indirect effects through capital deepening, education, and TFP, they found that the biggest impact operates through TFP. Interestingly, they also found a positive effect of country size on income, once the degree of openness was controlled for. This result suggests that among countries with similar degrees of openness, larger countries have higher income per capita. That is, there is a scale effect, as predicted by the "new" growth theory.

Using Frankel and Romer's IV methodology, Alesina, Spolaore, and Wacziarg (2003) found a positive effect of openness and scale on the growth *rate* of income per capita.[23] Moreover, they found that the two interact: in larger countries the same degree of openness has a smaller effect on growth and in more-open economies country size matters less.[24] These results are consistent with the theoretical observation that foreign trade provides access to world markets to small and large countries alike. Smaller countries gain more in terms of market-size expansion, and therefore the effect of trade on their income per capita and its rate of growth should be larger. Alesina, Spolaore, and Wacziarg found that a rise of one standard deviation in the degree of openness of a country the size of Mali (in population terms) would raise its growth rate by 0.419 percent. The same change in openness would raise the growth rate of a much smaller country, such as Seychelles, by 1.4 percent.[25] These are large effects indeed. But the effect of openness on growth peters out for countries the size of France. In such large economies additional trade does not contribute to economic growth.

These comparisons apply when other things are equal. But other things are not equal, of course. Countries differ in important dimensions that are not controlled for in this type of empirical work. For this reason the estimates are best interpreted as average impacts across countries. As we have seen, in countries with certain features trade accelerates growth, in countries with other features trade retards growth. A reasonable way to read this evidence is that on average the positive effects dominate.

## Evidence on Trade Policies

Trade volumes depend on endowments, technologies, preferences, and market structures, and on how these characteristics differ across countries. As a result, the trade volumes of some countries would be high and of others low even if all of them engaged in free trade. For this reason it is not apparent that growth rates should be positively correlated with trade volumes across countries. Moreover, even if one believed that trade promotes growth, one would not necessarily conclude from this premise that larger trade volumes promote faster growth. As a result, studies that examine correlations between growth rates and trade volumes cannot provide fully satisfactory evidence on the effects of trade on growth. It would have been more informative to study the mechanisms through which trade influences growth. But data limitations greatly restrict research of this type. As a result, growth economics—like many other areas of economics that face similar problems—has turned to the study of indirect relationships instead.

A great many studies have examined the impact of trade policies on growth. We have seen that growth theory does not predict a simple relationship between trade policies and growth. In some countries a restrictive trade policy may accelerate the growth of income per capita, in others it may slow it down. The way trade policy affects an economy's growth depends on the economy's characteristics, such as the type of products it trades on foreign markets or the human-capital intensity of its import-competing sectors. Nevertheless, empirical studies do not provide estimates of the growth effects of trade policies conditioned on these characteristics. Therefore estimates that exploit cross-country variations are best interpreted as average effects of trade policies on growth, similarly to the estimates of the effects of trade volumes on growth that were discussed above.

Bairoch (1993, chap. 4) argued that the European experience in the late nineteenth century does not support the view that protection is bad for growth. According to Bairoch, the liberal phase of European trade policies lasted from 1860 to 1892. In response to an inflow of cheap grain from Russia and the New

World, some countries raised their impediments to trade. France went protectionist in 1892. The growth rate of its GNP increased from an annual average of 1.2 percent in the decade preceding the policy shift to 1.3 percent in the decade following the policy shift. Germany changed its policy in 1885, experiencing a rise in the growth rate of its GNP from 1.3 percent in the decade preceding the rise of protection to 3.1 percent in the subsequent decade. Sweden also experienced an acceleration of GNP growth around its policy shift toward more protection in 1888, while Italy experienced a slowdown in GNP growth around 1887, the year in which it went protectionist. In view of this evidence Bairoch noted that "it remains generally true that in all countries (except Italy) the introduction of protectionist measures resulted in a distinct acceleration in economic growth during the first ten years following a change in policy, and that this took place regardless of when the measures were introduced" (1993, 50).

O'Rourke (2000) examined more carefully the relationship between average tariffs and growth in the late nineteenth century. Estimating a growth equation with data for ten countries between 1875 and 1914, he found a positive effect of tariffs on the rate of growth of real income per capita, thereby confirming Bairoch's argument.[26] Allowing for fixed country effects, his panel estimates imply that an increase of one standard deviation in the average tariff rate raised the annual growth rate by 0.74 percent.

Clemens and Williamson (2002) confirmed O'Rourke's finding for a sample of more than thirty countries between 1870 and 1913. But they also found that the relationship was reversed in the post–World War II period. That is, in the postwar period high-tariff countries grew more slowly than low-tariff countries.

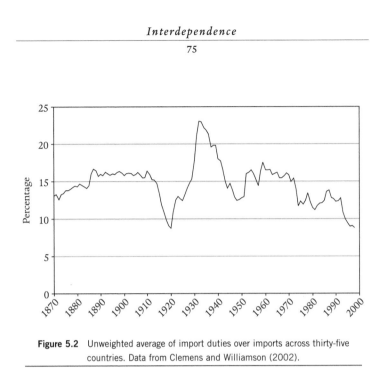

**Figure 5.2** Unweighted average of import duties over imports across thirty-five countries. Data from Clemens and Williamson (2002).

Clemens and Williamson suggested that the reversal might be related to the average level of protection in the world economy. When a country's trade partners have high tariffs, it can speed up its own growth by adopting a higher rate of protection. When a country's trade partners have low tariffs, however, higher protection harms growth.

Figure 5.2 portrays the evolution of the average tariff rate of thirty-five countries from the late nineteenth century to the late twentieth century.[27] Tariffs were higher before World War I than after World War II, and they hit record levels between the wars. This intertemporal pattern of tariffs is at the heart of Clemens and Williamson's explanation of the reversal of the relationship between protection and growth. Although they also provided econometric evidence in support of their hypothesis, note that in view of our theoretical discussion other interpretations of the evidence are possible as well.

The economies in the post–World War II period were very different from the economies in the late nineteenth century and the beginning of the twentieth century. In each of these eras there were important structural differences among countries. The structure of some countries could have produced a positive effect of tariffs on the growth of income per capita; the structure of others could have produced a negative effect. In each of these periods the econometric estimates measure the *average* response across countries of the growth rate to the rate of protection. Therefore we may interpret the evidence as stating that in the post–World War II period the channels through which protection hindered growth dominated, while in the late nineteenth century and the beginning of the twentieth century the channels through which protection promoted growth dominated. This is a reasonable interpretation, but it does not help to understand exactly what were the dominant channels of influence in each of these periods. An understanding of this issue requires studying the relationship between protection and growth *conditional* on the characteristics that affect the nature of this relationship.

Apart from these difficulties, the study of trade policies is also plagued by other hardships. Although in the late nineteenth century and the beginning of the twentieth century protection was predominantly in the form of tariffs, the nature of protection changed in the post–World War II period. As tariffs were reduced in the various negotiating rounds of the General Agreement on Tariffs and Trade (GATT), countries erected ever higher non-tariff barriers.[28] For this reason the average tariff rate displayed in Figure 5.2 does not provide an accurate measure of protection in the late twentieth century. This fact led scholars of the post-

World War II period to use a variety of additional indicators as proxies for levels of protection. These indicators include measures of real exchange-rate distortions, the size of the black-market premium on foreign exchange, the fraction of imports covered by nontariff barriers, and various institutional features of the economic regimes.[29] Other scholars used outcome indicators—such as the deviation of trade volumes from the predictions of trade theory—to measure the restrictiveness of trade regimes.[30] They all found negative effects of trade restrictions on growth.

There are nagging problems with these studies. Many of the problems were discussed by Rodríguez and Rodrik (2000). Trade policies are not entirely exogenous, they are often highly correlated with other policies, and they are too complex to be adequately represented by a single index of trade restrictiveness. The Sachs-Warner index is a good example (see Sachs and Warner 1995). It is a binary index, which assigned the value 1 when an economy was deemed to be open and 0 when it was deemed to be closed. An economy was considered to be closed if its average tariff exceeded 40 percent, or nontariff barriers covered more than 40 percent of its imports, or it had a socialist economic system, or much of its exports were controlled by a state monopoly, or its black-market premium exceeded 20 percent during the 1970s or the 1980s.

The Sachs-Warner index was found to be positively correlated with the growth rate of income per capita. According to the estimates, countries that were open grew faster—at a rate of 2.44 percent per annum—than countries that were closed. This impact is large indeed. As Rodríguez and Rodrik showed, however, the Sachs-Warner index is dominated by the criteria applied to state monopolies and the black-market premium. At the same time, black-market premiums are highly correlated with other government policies. Black-market premiums tend to be high in countries with lax macroeconomic policies, tight capital and exchange controls, and high levels of corruption. For this reason the estimated impact of this index on growth may not properly isolate the effects of trade policies, but may rather reflect the broader impact of government policies on economic growth.

Wacziarg (2001) corroborated this hypothesis. He developed a simultaneous equations model that allowed him to estimate the impact of trade policies on growth via six different channels: the quality of macroeconomic policies, the size of government, price distortions, factor accumulation, technology transmission, and foreign direct investment. That is, he estimated the effects on growth of the variables representing the six channels, as well as the effects of trade policies on each one of these variables.[31] Combining these estimates enabled him to assess the impact of trade policies on growth.

In the first stage Wacziarg estimated the impact of average tariffs, the nontariff coverage ratios, and the timing of trade liberalization according to the Sachs-Warner index, on the trade shares. He also estimated this equation without the timing of trade-liberalization variables. He then used the predicted impact of the trade-policy variables on the trade share as a measure of the restrictiveness of trade policies, in order to estimate its impact on the variables representing the various channels of influence on economic growth. When he used the timing of trade liberalization based on the Sachs-Warner index, he found that 63 percent of the effects of trade policies on growth were through investment, with technology transmission and the quality of macroeconomic policies constituting the other two important channels of transmission. Without the timing variables of trade liberalization based on the Sachs-Warner index, the effects of trade policies through the quality of macroeconomic policies disappear. In terms of the overall impact, Wacziarg estimated that in this case an increase of one standard deviation in the restrictiveness of trade policies reduces the growth rate of income per capita by 0.264 percent annually, a significant impact.

My view is that despite the many difficulties that exist in the literature, it is fair to conclude that the evidence favors a negative effect of protection on rates of growth in the post–World War II period. Importantly, there is no real evidence of a positive link for this era. But I also share the view expressed by Rodríguez and Rodrik that "it might be productive to look for *contingent* relationships between trade policy and growth. Do trade restrictions operate differently in low- vs. high-income countries? In small vs. large countries? In countries with a comparative advantage in primary products vs. those with comparative advantage in manufactured goods?" (2000, 317). To this list of contingencies I would only add structural features, which have been found in theoretical models to affect the link between trade policies and growth.

## Evidence on Research and Development

Finally, consider the international spillover of knowledge. This link turns out to be critical for the understanding of divergence forces in the world economy. As I have argued, the theoretical models show that when useful knowledge of this type—emanating from R&D—diffuses to foreign countries at the same speed as it diffuses within the domestic economy, then these knowledge flows provide a potent force of convergence in the world economy. If, however, the international flows are slow relative to the domestic flows, then these knowledge flows provide a potent force of divergence. In particular, in an extreme case in which no international flows of knowledge take place, a country that has an initial advantage in innovative activities widens its advantage over time. Such a country dominates the high-technology sector in the long run, and its residents enjoy a higher standard of living. In contrast, a country that starts with a disadvantage in R&D is thrust into specialization in traditional goods, and such a country ends up with a lower standard of living.

But it is important to note that a lagging country need not lose from advances made by a leading country. It can, for example, benefit from the new products invented by the technological leader if the countries trade with each other. Nevertheless, such a country lags behind in its level of development.

This line of reasoning suggests that it is extremely important to evaluate the extent to which international spillovers of knowledge exist, the more so in view of the fact that more than 95 percent of the world's R&D is carried out by a handful of industrial countries. If, for example, the R&D performed by these industrial countries enhanced their common knowledge stock but did not feed knowledge into the less-developed countries, then international R&D spillovers would provide a major force of divergence between the rich North and the poor South.

A large number of empirical studies have examined this issue. Building on the work of Griliches (1979), they used R&D capital stocks as measures of the stocks of knowledge. A country's domestic R&D capital stock is constructed in the same way as its stock of regular capital—that is, by starting from a benchmark stock in the distant past and by adding on investment net of depreciation. In the case of R&D capital the investment consists of R&D investment, while depreciation is taken to be 15 percent

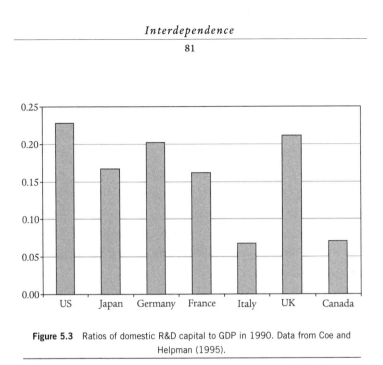

**Figure 5.3** Ratios of domestic R&D capital to GDP in 1990. Data from Coe and Helpman (1995).

annually or less.[32] Figure 5.3 depicts the ratios of domestic R&D capital stocks to GDP in 1990 for the G7 countries. While in the United States, Germany, and the UK the domestic R&D capital stocks were in excess of 20 percent of GDP, they were smaller in Japan and France, and particularly small in Italy and Canada. The low ratios in Italy and Canada reflect low levels of invest-ment in R&D that are documented in Figure 4.2. There were thus substantial variations in the domestic R&D capital stocks across the G7 countries. These variations were even larger across the entire sample of twenty-two countries used by Coe and Help-man (1995). The average ratio was below $\frac{1}{5}$ in the G7 countries, but was slightly below $\frac{1}{10}$ in the other fifteen countries.

Coe and Helpman (1995) estimated the effects of domestic as well as foreign R&D capital stocks on the productivity level of every country in their sample. For this purpose a *foreign* R&D

capital stock was constructed as a weighted average of the domestic R&D capital stocks of the country's trade partners, using trade shares as weights. The idea behind this weighting scheme was that the impact of a trade partner's R&D is larger the more important the partner is in the country's international trade. In addition to foreign and domestic capital stocks, Coe and Helpman also estimated the effect of the degree of a country's openness to foreign trade on its productivity, allowing trade openness to interact with the foreign R&D capital stock—that is, allowing larger impacts of overall trade on countries with larger foreign R&D capital stocks.

This methodology allowed Coe and Helpman to explain roughly 60 percent of the variation across countries in TFP levels. And they found that the elasticity of TFP with respect to the domestic R&D capital stock was about three times higher in the G7 countries than in the smaller industrial countries. Computing rates of return to investment in R&D from these elasticities, they found rates of 85 percent in the small industrial countries and 120 percent in the large industrial countries.[33] Moreover, R&D in the G7 countries produced an additional return of 30 percent in the smaller industrial countries, thereby revealing substantial R&D spillovers across national boarders. Finally, these authors found that trade openness had a significant impact on productivity. More-open economies were more productive, and the larger a country's foreign R&D capital stock, the larger its productivity gains.[34]

The Coe-Helpman methodology for estimating the impact of foreign R&D capital stocks on total factor productivity was applied to seventy-seven developing countries by Coe, Helpman, and Hoffmaister (1997). Although these developing countries performed negligible amounts of R&D themselves, the question was whether they benefited from the R&D performed in the industrial countries. The study showed that these effects were substantial, and that foreign R&D capital stocks explained 20 percent of the variation in the TFP levels of the developing countries.[35]

Although this methodology was criticized by various authors, the main finding—that R&D capital stocks of trade partners have a noticeable impact on a country's total factor productivity—appears to be robust.[36] Moreover, other factors, such as the extent of foreign direct investment, were found to provide measurable impacts on the degree to which countries benefit from foreign research and development.[37] Keller (2001) decomposed the international R&D spillovers into three parts: trade, FDI, and language skills. He found that close to 70 percent of the effect was due to trade, about 15 percent due to FDI, and another 15 percent due to language skills.[38]

To quantify the impact of R&D on growth trajectories, Bayoumi, Coe, and Helpman (1999) incorporated into the MULTIMOD model of the International Monetary Fund the spillover equations that Coe and Helpman (1995) and Coe, Helpman, and Hoffmaister (1997) estimated. MULTIMOD is an econometric model of the world economy that has been used by the IMF for medium-term forecasting. The model has long-run neoclassical features, and it covers the most important regions of the world. The IMF treats the rate of technological change as exogenous, however. By embedding these equations into the model Bayoumi, Coe, and Helpman were able to endogenize the rate of TFP growth. They then used the model to simulate the effects of various expansions in R&D investment on the growth of countries and regions of the world.

Figure 5.4 depicts the long-run outcome, which takes about

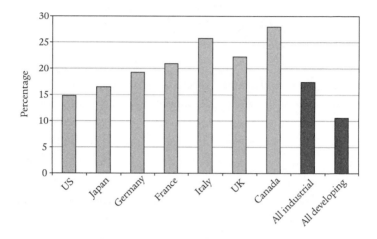

**Figure 5.4** Long-run output gains from an expansion of R&D by 1/2 percent of GDP in twenty-one industrial countries. Data from Bayoumi, Coe, and Helpman (1999).

eighty years to attain, of a coordinated permanent expansion of R&D investment by ½ percent of GDP in each one of twenty-one industrial countries. The U.S. output grows by 15 percent, while Canada's and Italy's output expands by more than 25 percent. On average the output of all the industrial countries rises by 17.5 percent. And importantly, the output of all the less-developed countries rises by 10.6 percent on average. That is, the less-developed countries experience substantial gains from R&D expansion in the industrial countries.

The growth in final output results from a combination of TFP growth and capital accumulation. As productivity rises, it stimulates more investment in capital, which raises the capital-labor ratio. For both reasons output grows. About two-thirds of the growth was directly due to productivity, and the remaining third was due to the induced accumulation of capital.

It is encouraging to see how much less-developed countries benefit from R&D in the industrial countries. These benefits are even larger when measured in consumption rather than GDP units, because larger levels of R&D in the industrial countries bring about terms-of-trade improvements in the less-developed countries. Nevertheless, these results also have a discouraging side: they show that investment in innovation widens the gap between rich and poor countries. The output gains of the industrial countries exceed the output gains of the less-developed countries. We therefore conclude that investment in innovation in the industrial countries leads to divergence of income between the North and the South.

# 6

## INEQUALITY

I next turn to the relationship between income in-equality and economic growth. We examined the inequality of income per capita across countries in Chapter 1, noticing that this type of inequality has increased over time. In particular, the gap between the rich North and the poor South has widened in the post–World War II period. And in the previous chapter we discussed a variety of mechanisms that could explain these developments.

Now we focus on the personal distribution of income. Our main questions are: Does the distribution of income within a country affect its growth rate? And does economic growth affect the distribution of income?

Kuznets (1955, 1963) suggested that the personal distribution of income may change in a systematic way along a country's development path. Using a small sample of countries, five in the earlier study and eighteen in the later, he noted that among the low-income countries income distribution was more unequal in the relatively richer countries, while among the high-income countries the distribution of income was more unequal in the relatively poorer countries in the group. Using this evidence he suggested that in the early stages of development rising income per capita leads to a worsening of the distribution of income, while in the late stages of development rising income per capita leads to an improvement in the distribution of income.[1] This became known as the *Kuznets Curve*—an inverted U-shape relationship between income per capita and personal income inequality.

Early studies supported Kuznets's hypothesis.[2] But they were plagued with data problems, and they relied on cross-country variations, with no direct evidence on the evolution of within-country inequality over time.[3] The construction of a comprehensive data set on income inequality by Deininger and Squire (1996) enabled researchers to reassess the Kuznets hypothesis, utilizing variations of inequality and growth rates across countries as well as variations over time within countries. The results from these studies appear to be negative. That is, there is no Kuznets Curve: development does not appear to first worsen and then improve the distribution of income.[4] I therefore center the discussion in this chapter on the effects of inequality on growth and on the effects of growth on inequality.

Bourguignon and Morrisson (2002) studied the evolution of inequality in the world's distribution of personal income since 1820. After reporting a large number of inequality indicators, they noted: "Over the 172 years considered here, the mean income of world inhabitants increased by a factor of 7.6. The mean income of the bottom 20 percent increased only by a factor of slightly more than 3, that of the bottom 60 percent by about 4, and that of the top decile by almost 10. At the same time, however, the extreme poverty headcount fell from 84 percent of the world population in 1820 to 24 percent in 1992" (2002, 733). Ev-

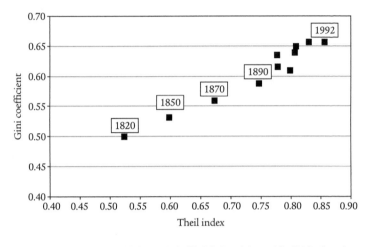

**Figure 6.1**   The Gini coefficient and the Theil index of the world's distribution of personal income, 1820–1992. Data from Bourguignon and Morrisson (2002).

idently the massive growth of the world economy has been unevenly distributed, but it has greatly benefited both the top and the bottom income earners.

Among the many income inequality measures, such as the ratio of the income of the top decile to the income of the bottom decile, the Gini coefficient and the Theil index are among the most widely used. Both equal zero when income is evenly distributed, and they rise as incomes become more unequal.[5] Figure 6.1 depicts the relationship between the Gini coefficient and the Theil index of the world's distribution of personal income, from the early part of the nineteenth century to the late part of the twentieth century. As the figure shows, these indexes are highly correlated—that is, they represent similar trends over time.

Although economists seem to prefer the Gini coefficient,

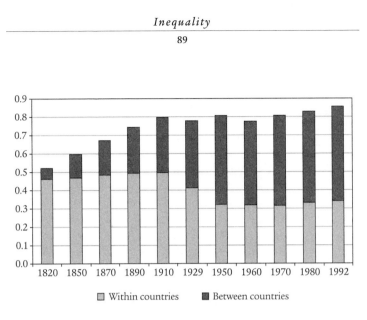

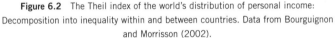

**Figure 6.2** The Theil index of the world's distribution of personal income: Decomposition into inequality within and between countries. Data from Bourguignon and Morrisson (2002).

the Theil index is more convenient for decompositions of the sources of inequality.[6] A decomposition of the inequality in the personal distribution of income into within-country and between-country inequality, due to Bourguignon and Morrisson, is presented in Figure 6.2. The first thing to note is that inequality increased rapidly during the nineteenth century and less so during the twentieth century. Second, inequality within countries declined substantially during the early part of the twentieth century, and rose slightly in the post–World War II period. Inequality between countries, however, was particularly large in the postwar period. Figure 6.3 shows the fraction of total inequality that is attributable to inequality within countries. This fraction declined rapidly during the nineteenth century and the first half of the twentieth century, and remained relatively stable in the

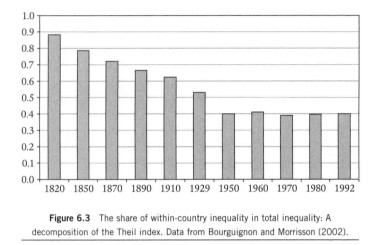

**Figure 6.3** The share of within-country inequality in total inequality: A decomposition of the Theil index. Data from Bourguignon and Morrisson (2002).

postwar period. This suggests that during the postwar period, until 1992, inequality trends were similar within and between countries.

Comparing Figures 6.2 and 1.5, we see that the rise in inequality in the nineteenth century took place during a period of rapid acceleration in the world's growth. In contrast, the acceleration in growth in the post–World War II period was not accompanied by a major rise in inequality. Worldwide trends do not exhibit a clear-cut relationship between inequality and growth. The question that arises, however, is whether these broad averages mask variations across countries that do exhibit clear patterns.

## Effects of Inequality on Growth

Does inequality within a country slow its growth? This important question has only a tentative answer.

Conflicting forces shape the relationship between the degree of inequality and the growth rate of income per capita. First, consider savings. If, as Kaldor (1955–56) argued, the propensity to save is higher from profits than from wage income, then a redistribution of income from wages to profits raises aggregate savings. Or if the marginal propensity to save of high-income individuals is higher than the marginal propensity to save of low-income individuals, then a redistribution of income from low-income to high-income individuals raises aggregate savings.[7] These redistributions raise inequality. But by raising savings they also raise investment and thereby the growth of GDP.[8] Under the circumstances less equal societies should grow faster.

Second, inequality may retard growth as a result of credit constraints. Frictions in capital markets, which result from informational asymmetries or institutional constraints, are prevalent in developing countries. They limit the borrowing capacity of individuals who have no tangible assets, because these individuals cannot provide collateral for their loans. As a result, these individuals cannot undertake investment projects, whether in physical or in human capital, that entail costs in excess of their borrowing limitations. In these circumstances aggregate investment is affected by the distribution of assets. Substantial inequality in the ownership of assets reduces aggregate investment, because the disadvantaged individuals are prevented from undertaking profitable investment projects. In societies with a more even distribution of asset ownership, more profitable investment projects get funded. As a result, the more equal societies invest more and grow faster.[9]

Third, inequality breeds redistribution. Political decisions in democratic societies are often approximated in economic and political models by the most preferred policy of the median voter.[10] In unequal societies the median voter has a preference for income redistribution, because in these societies the median income is below the average. As a result, taxes and transfers are used to redistribute income from the well-to-do to the less fortunate members of society. Since the available taxes and transfers are distortionary, however, this redistribution may slow growth.[11]

Alesina and Rodrik (1994) and Persson and Tabellini (1994) showed that for a cross section of countries the data support a negative correlation between the degree of income inequality and the subsequent growth of income per capita. Controlling for initial income per capita and the level of education, as in Barro (1991), Alesina and Rodrik found a significant negative effect of the Gini coefficient of the distribution of income on the growth rate. But they also found that this effect becomes insignificant when the Gini coefficient of the distribution of land ownership is also included as an explanatory variable.[12] In other words, inequality in the ownership of land not only is more important for explaining growth than inequality in the distribution of income, it also turns the distribution of income into an inconsequential factor in the growth equation. This finding has been corroborated by Deininger and Squire (1998) with better inequality data and a larger sample of countries. They showed that income distribution has an insignificant effect on growth not only when the inequality in the distribution of land ownership is accounted for, but also when regional differences in growth rates are allowed for.[13] Moreover, the same regional differences in growth rates did not eliminate the explanatory power of inequality in the ownership of land.[14]

Alesina and Rodrik (1994) also reported the impact of democracy on growth. If a political process of redistribution through the median voter were at work, one would expect the effect of inequality to be particularly strong in democracies. But these authors were not able to identify a significant role for democracy in the relationship between inequality and growth. This issue was reexamined by Deininger and Squire (1998). They estimated separate equations for the countries with democratic regimes and the countries with nondemocratic regimes. And they found that the Gini coefficient of inequality in land ownership had no significant effect on the subsequent economic growth of democracies and a negative effect on nondemocratic regimes. Inequality in income had no significant effect in both samples of countries. This evidence casts doubt on the importance of the redistribution mechanism in which the median voter plays a central role.[15]

Barro (2000) noted, however, that income inequality appears to affect the growth rates of different countries differentially, depending on their level of development. He showed that more income inequality reduces the growth rate of low-income countries but raises the growth rate of high-income countries. A possible conclusion from this evidence is that credit constraints are important in low-income but not in high-income countries. To test this hypothesis, Barro estimated the impact of the product of the Gini coefficient of income and a measure of the financial development of a country on the growth rate.[16] He found that this variable had no significant effect on growth.

My tentative conclusion is that inequality slows growth.[17] The research in this area has, however, not been able to identify the mechanisms through which this happens. In particular, there is no convincing evidence that the preferences of the median voter retard growth via the political demand for redistribution, or that credit market constraints have a significant impact on this relationship. Therefore, although we can argue with limited confidence that inequality within a country slows its growth, we cannot say much about the channels through which this influence plays out.

## Sources of Inequality

Income inequality evolves in response to a host of forces, economic growth being only one of them. And even when growth changes the distribution of income, the ways in which it affects the distribution depend on the sources of growth. For this reason it is difficult to isolate the effects of growth on inequality, and this relationship needs to be examined in specific contexts rather than in general terms.

The evolution of wage inequality, which played a major role in shaping the U.S. distribution of income, is a case in point. Average U.S. real wages have not changed much between the late 1970s and the mid-1990s; however, real wages of high-wage workers increased while real wages of low-wage workers declined.[18] This trend was reflected in a rising *college wage premium,* that is, a rising wage of college graduates relative to the wage of workers with no college education. During the same period the supply of workers with a college degree increased substantially relative to the supply of workers with lower education, as can be seen in Figure 6.4, but this growth in the relative labor supply of college graduates did not depress their relative wage.[19] As a result of these changes, the entire distribution of wages became more unequal, as can be seen from the time pattern of the Gini coefficient of the wage distribution in Figure 6.5.

The rising wage gap between high-wage and low-wage workers was not unique to the United States. Katz and Autor (1999, table 10) reported widening gaps between 90th percentile earners and 10th percentile earners from the late 1970s to the mid-1990s in

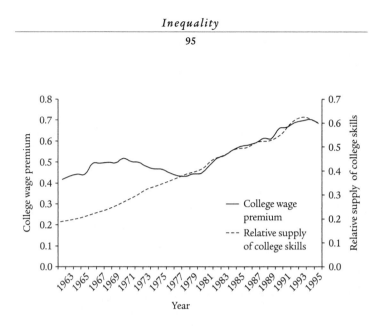

**Figure 6.4**   U.S. college wage premium and the relative supply of skills. Data from Acemoglu (2002a).

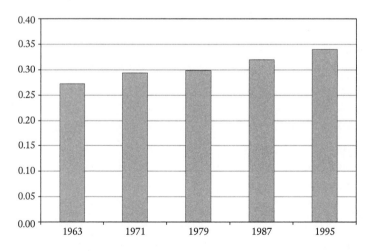

**Figure 6.5**   The Gini coefficient of the U.S. distribution of wages of full-time, full-year male and female workers. Data from Katz and Autor (1999).

most OECD countries. True, in the United States the gap increased by 29 percent, more than in any other country. But it also increased by 27 percent in the UK, 15 percent in New Zealand, 14 percent in Italy, and 9 percent in Canada. In some countries the widening was small: 3 percent in the Netherlands and 1 percent in France. Only in two countries did the gap narrow: by 4 percent in Norway and 6 percent in Germany. Wage inequality thus increased throughout most of the OECD.

A large literature has sought to explain these developments.[20] Most of it has focused on two competing explanations: the integration of less-developed countries into the world's trading system and the direction of technological change.[21]

The trade argument begins by noting that less-developed countries have a relatively large supply of unskilled workers. As a result, they specialize in industries that are relatively unskilled-labor intensive. Consequently, their integration into the world's trading system from the late 1970s to the mid-1990s increased the relative supply of products that were unskilled-labor intensive, thereby depressing their relative price. The decline in the relative price of these products changed the relative demand for inputs in the advanced countries in favor of skilled workers, because it became more profitable to produce skill-intensive products. This shift in labor demand increased the wage of skilled workers relative to the wage of unskilled workers. Moreover, the wages of the unskilled declined.[22] This explains the rise in the college wage premium and the decline in the real wage of low-skill workers.[23]

The technology argument notes the rise of skill-biased technological change since the late 1970s. Changes in production techniques based on digitally controlled machines, organizational change in the workplace (enabled by the availability of personal computers and information technology), and the fast decline of the relative price of computer services all worked to raise the relative demand for skilled workers. As a result, the relative wage of these workers increased.[24]

Krugman (1995) argued persuasively that the nature and extent of U.S. trade with less-developed countries cannot explain the large increase in the college wage premium. Although in theory the integration of less-developed countries into the world's trading system could increase the relative wage of skilled workers in the industrial countries, existing estimates of key parameters, such as the elasticity of substitution in production between skilled and unskilled workers, imply that it cannot explain the *magnitude* of the observed increase. In Krugman's view, technological change played a major role.[25]

Leamer (2000) argued instead that skill-biased technological change cannot be the correct explanation, because in a country that faces given world prices, skill-biased technological change acts like an expansion of the supply of skill, and therefore leads to a reallocation of resources from less to more skill-intensive sectors, with no effect on the remuneration of effective units of inputs. That is, skill-biased technological change does not affect the wage rate of unskilled workers, and it raises the wage rate of skilled workers in proportion to the rate of technical change. Leamer pointed out that what matters for the relative remuneration of effective units of inputs is the sector bias of technological change rather than the factor bias. In particular, if productivity rises in skill-intensive sectors only, be it as a result of skill-biased or Hicks-neutral technological change, then the relative remuneration of skilled workers rises. And if productivity rises in sectors that are unskilled-labor intensive, then the relative remuneration of effective units of skilled labor declines.[26]

Although Leamer's arguments are theoretically correct, Krugman (2000) pointed out that they are of limited use in the debate, because they rely on the assumption that technological change does not influence world prices. This would be a suitable assumption if, say, the technology were to improve in one country only, and that country were small relative to the world economy. But if the improvements in technology are worldwide or in the industrial countries, which jointly produce most of the world's output, it is not appropriate to assume that prices do not respond to technological change. Under these circumstances technological change has a direct impact on relative wages for given prices, and an indirect impact through price movements that respond to shifts in supply. Using a simple two-sector, two-factor model of international trade with fixed expenditure shares, Krugman showed that in this type of world Hicks-neutral technological progress, possibly at different rates in the two sectors, does not change the relative remuneration of effective units of skilled and unskilled labor. But when the elasticity of substitution between the inputs is low, skill-biased technological change raises the relative remuneration of an effective unit of skill, independently of whether the technological improvement takes place in the skill-intensive or the unskilled-labor–intensive sector.

Is there evidence in support of the technology explanation? Direct evidence of skill-biased technological change exists in the form of positive correlations between various indicators of technology and the within-industry growth of the employment share of skilled workers and their cost share. In these studies, R&D expenditure, the employment of scientists and engineers, and investment in computer technology are used to measure technological intensity.[27] But the most striking evidence, which is indirect, concerns the shift in the relative employment of skilled workers in various industries across countries. An increase in the relative wage of skilled workers implies that cost-minimizing producers will shift employment away from skilled workers toward the unskilled. Therefore, in the absence of skill-biased technological change, we would observe a rising employment of unskilled versus skilled workers in all industries of the countries in which the relative wage of skilled workers increased. This has not happened, however. As Berman, Bound, and Machin (1998) have shown,

> Across countries with very diverse labor market institutions, two common features stand out. (1) The increased use of nonproduction [that is, skilled] workers in manufacturing is a universal phenomenon . . . [T]heir proportion increased by an average of four percentage points in the 1970s and three percentage points in the 1980s. (2) In all these countries the vast majority of the aggregate substitution toward nonproduction workers was due to substitution toward nonproduction workers *within* industries in both decades. (1257)

Figure 6.6 presents the contribution of the within-industry changes in employment to the increased percentage of nonproduction workers in manufacturing industries, which took place in the 1970s and the 1980s, measured as a share of the increased percentage. It shows that more than half of the changes were within industries, and that for most of the countries this share was well above one-half.[28] Moreover, the correlations across countries between industries in which the proportion of skilled workers increased were generally positive. Skill upgrading within industries was thus pervasive in the industrial countries, which

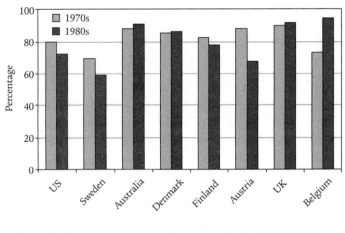

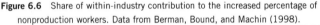

**Figure 6.6** Share of within-industry contribution to the increased percentage of nonproduction workers. Data from Berman, Bound, and Machin (1998).

supports Krugman's argument that technological change was worldwide. Under these circumstances Krugman's analysis is more suitable than Leamer's.[29]

Although the studies of skill upgrading within and across industries provide convincing evidence that the wage inequality in the industrial countries did not increase only due to trade with less-developed countries, and that skill-biased technological change played an important role in these wage developments, they fall short of providing a quantitative assessment of the relative importance of these competing explanations. Borjas, Freeman, and Katz (1997) do provide such an assessment. They used the factor content of the growth of U.S. trade with less-developed countries between 1980 and 1995 to calculate the implicit rise, caused by this trade, in the supply of workers with high school education relative to the supply of workers with college education.[30] Then they calculated the impact of these supply changes on the relative wage of these groups of workers, using an elasticity of substitution of 1.4 between them in production.[31] The resulting change in relative wages turned out to be about one-fifth of the actual rise in the college wage premium. That is, according to Borjas, Freeman, and Katz, the expansion of trade with less-developed countries accounts for only 20 percent of the rise in the U.S. college wage premium, while the remaining 80 percent is attributed to other factors, such as the growth in the relative supply of college skills, depicted in Figure 6.4, and skill-biased technological change. According to their model, the rise in the relative supply of college skills reduced the college wage premium. Nevertheless, one contributor to this trend, immigration, worked in the opposite direction. That is, by expanding the supply of workers with a high school education (or lower), immigration raised the college wage premium. According to their estimates, this impact was similar in size to the expansion of trade with less-developed countries.

Feenstra and Hanson (2003) argued, however, that the contribution to U.S. wage inequality of U.S. trade with less-developed countries is significantly larger than one-fifth, simply as a result of the fact that the *nature* of this trade has changed. In particular, while the theory behind this estimate implicitly assumes that the United States and less-developed countries exchange primarily final goods, trade in intermediate inputs has grown tremendously. And expanding trade in intermediate inputs can prompt a rise in the college wage premium even at constant final good prices.[32]

The theoretical argument proceeds as follows. Declining barriers to trade and technological developments have enabled American companies to shift the stages of production of activities that are unskilled-labor intensive to less-developed countries.[33] The first to move were the least skill-intensive activities. As a result, the relative demand for skilled workers increased in the United States, thereby bidding up the college wage premium. Moreover, since the least skill-intensive activities in the United States still employed a ratio of skilled to unskilled labor that exceeded the average ratio of skilled to unskilled labor in the less-developed countries, the reallocation of these activities to the less-developed countries also increased their relative demand for skilled workers. Similar arguments apply to other industrial countries. Therefore, the skill premium increased both in the North and in the South.[34]

Using variations across U.S. manufacturing industries, Feenstra and Hanson (2003) estimated the contribution of purchases of foreign intermediate inputs (what they called "outsourcing") and the share of computers in the capital stock (a measure of technological supremacy) to the rise of the relative wage of skilled workers. The results proved to be sensitive to the valuation of computers. They reported:

> Over the 1979–1990 period, outsourcing accounts for 15 percent of the increase in the relative wage of nonproduction workers, and computers measured using *ex post* rental prices account for 35 percent of this increase; thus, computers are twice as important as outsourcing. When instead the computer share of the capital stock is measured using *ex ante* rental prices, then outsourcing explains about 25 percent while computers explain about 20 percent of the increase in the nonproduction/production wage. Finally, when the computer share of the capital

> stock is replaced with the computer share of *investment*,
> then the contribution of outsourcing falls to about 10
> percent, while the contribution of computers rises so
> much that it explains the *entire* increase in the relative
> wage. (Feenstra and Hanson 2003, 173)

Although the international fragmentation of production contributed significantly to the rise in the relative wage of skilled
workers, technological progress was apparently more important.
And if one takes the view that the bulk of the weight in the ac-
quisition of computers should be attached to the most recent
investments, then one is led to conclude that technological progress had the dominant impact on the evolution of wage inequality.[35]

Finally, it has been suggested that capital accumulation has
increased wage inequality. This argument starts by noting that
capital and skill complement each other in the production process, while capital and unskilled labor substitute for each other.
That is, the elasticity of substitution between capital and skilled
labor is low while the elasticity of substitution between capital
and unskilled labor is high.[36] Under these circumstances capital
accumulation raises the marginal product of skilled workers and
reduces the marginal product of the unskilled. Therefore capital
accumulation can explain a rising college wage premium and a
declining real wage of the unskilled.

Krusell and colleagues (2000) followed this route by decomposing capital into equipment and structures, and by construct-
ing a model in which capital equipment is a complement to
educated workers and a substitute to uneducated workers. They
estimated the parameters of this model from U.S. data and

showed that the model tracks well the U.S. relative wage movements over three decades, from 1960 to 1990. In this view capital accumulation explains most of the rise in wage inequality.[37]

One should note, however, that this conclusion rests on the growth of capital equipment, which was driven during the critical period of the widening wage gap by a rapid decline in equipment prices. And this decline in equipment prices resulted from technological progress.[38] Therefore one way to interpret these findings is that there was technology-skill complementarity that was mediated by capital equipment. This interpretation is in line with the findings of Goldin and Katz (1998), who reported that during most of the twentieth century technological progress was complementary to skill.

Moreover, the findings of Krusell and his colleagues were challenged by Ruiz-Arranz (n.d.). She decomposed equipment into information technology (IT) equipment and non-IT equipment, and estimated a translog production function which allows more flexible forms of substitutability across inputs than the Krusell et al. formulation. And she found that capital-skill complementarity takes the form of complementarity between IT capital and skills, but not between non-IT capital and skills. As a result, the fast growth of IT equipment increased the skill premium while the growth of non-IT equipment narrowed it. Since the accumulation of IT equipment is related to technological change, these results support the view that technological change is responsible for the widening wage gap between skilled and unskilled workers.[39]

Acemoglu (1998) proposed a mechanism that generates skill-biased technological change in countries with a rising relative supply of skilled workers, which in turn helps to explain the evolution of the wage gap. In his model, technological change can be directed toward inputs that are used with skilled labor or toward inputs that are used with unskilled labor. An increase in the relative supply of skilled workers then has two effects. On the one hand, it raises the relative supply of skill-intensive products, thereby depressing their relative price. This reduces the incentive to improve inputs that work with skilled labor. On the other hand, the larger quantity of skilled labor has a positive size effect, and improvements in the inputs that work with skilled labor become more valuable. This raises the incentive to invest in improving skill-related inputs. On balance, the size effect dominates, and an expansion in the relative supply of skilled workers biases technological change in favor of skilled workers.[40] Acemoglu (2003) showed that international trade produces a similar bias. Therefore, as argued by Wood (1994), international trade can affect relative wages through induced technological change. Unfortunately, there are no good assessments of the size of this effect.

## The Poor

The effects of growth on the poorest members of society are controversial. Has growth been harmful to the poor, as some have argued? Or has the growth tide raised all boats, as others have argued?

We have seen that the world's distribution of personal income became more unequal over time, starting with the early part of the nineteenth century (see Figure 6.1). This development is also manifested in the decline over time in the income share of the bottom quintile of the population, as depicted in Figure 6.7, which shows that the income share of the poorest quintile declined from 4.7 percent in 1820 to 2.2 percent in 1992. The big-

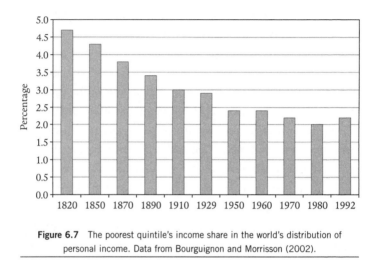

**Figure 6.7** The poorest quintile's income share in the world's distribution of personal income. Data from Bourguignon and Morrisson (2002).

gest decline occurred in the nineteenth century, and there was little change in the post–World War II period.

Data of this sort do not provide a complete characterization of the conditions of the poor, however, because these data depict changes in their relative position only. Alternatively one can ask whether poverty, measured in terms of a threshold of real income, has grown or declined over time. Figure 6.8 describes the evolution of two such measures: the fraction of the world's population that lives on less than $1 a day and the fraction of the world's population that lives on less than $2 dollars a day, where the purchasing power of each dollar is held constant in terms of 1985 prices.[41] Both poverty rates declined over time, and the fraction of people in extreme poverty, that is, those with less than $1 a day, declined rapidly in the post–World War II period.[42] It fol-

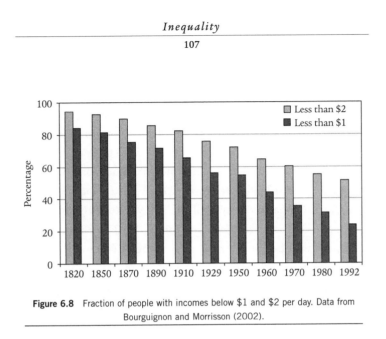

**Figure 6.8** Fraction of people with incomes below $1 and $2 per day. Data from Bourguignon and Morrisson (2002).

lows that the Golden Age of economic growth admitted substantial poverty reduction.

The number of people affected by this decline in poverty is staggering. In 1970, according to Sala-i-Martin (2002), 1,324 million people lived on less than $2 a day and 554 million lived on less than $1 a day. Between 1970 and 1998 the number of people who lived on less than $2 a day declined by 350 million; the number of people who lived in extreme poverty, on less than $1 a day, declined by 201 million. And these changes took place during a period of rapid population growth.

The fast economic growth of China and India, two countries that account for one-third of the world's population, contributed to the world's poverty reduction in a major way.[43] The Summers-Heston data set PWT 5.6 implies that between 1980 and 1992 China's real income per capita grew at an average annual rate of 3.58 percent and India's grew at 3.12 percent. These growth rates were much higher than the U.S. growth rate in the same period, which was only 1.33 percent. According to Quah's (2002) estimates, the fraction of people who lived on less than $2 a day declined in China from a range of 37–54 percent in 1980 to 14–17 percent in 1992, and it declined in India from 48–62 percent in 1980 to 12–19 percent in 1992. While the population increased in China from 981 million in 1980 to 1,162 million in 1992, and in India from 687 million in 1980 to 884 million in 1992, the number of poor people declined in China from 360–530 million in 1980 to 158–192 million in 1992, and in India from 326–426 million in 1980 to 110–166 million 1992. The economic growth of China and India was associated with massive poverty reductions. Is this pattern special to these countries or is it more general?

Dollar and Kraay (2002) showed that China and India are not special cases. Using a large sample of countries with observations in the postwar period, they showed that the average real income per capita of a country's poorest quintile moved practically one-to-one with the average real income per capita of the country's entire population. This relationship, which is very tight, is depicted in Figure 6.9.[44] Dollar and Kraay also showed that an almost one-to-one relationship existed between the growth rates of these variables, although data limitations forced them to estimate this slope for a smaller sample of countries. Finally, these researchers examined the effects on the average income of the poor of certain variables that are known to influence countries' growth rates. They found that these variables had no disproportional effect on the real income of the poor. That is, the influence of these variables was orthogonal to income distribution, and

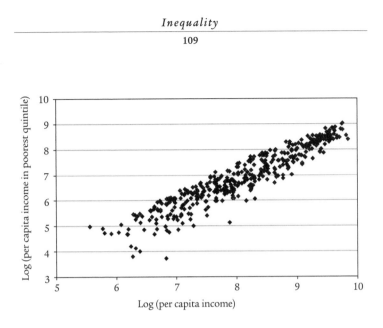

**Figure 6.9** The relationship between the average income per capita of the poorest quintile and the average income per capita in 137 countries. Data from Dollar and Kraay (2002).

they affected the poor in the same way that they affected the average person.[45]

In summary, although cross-country evidence of this sort may not prove that growth raises all incomes proportionately, it is hard not to conclude from it that on average growth has raised the income of the poor around the world.[46] We know, of course, of countries in which the poor did not do well during growth episodes, the United States from the mid-1970s to the mid-1990s being one of them. But the question remains, What are the mechanisms that link growth to income distribution, and which of them are particularly important? Can the economic system be organized in ways that encourage growth, and the growth of income for the poorest members of society in particular? What role do institutions play in this process? And which economic and political institutions are particularly important? Most of these questions are waiting for answers. Some of the issues that arise in considering them are discussed in the next chapter.

# 7

## INSTITUTIONS AND POLITICS

After we account for the accumulation of inputs, large differences in income per capita remain across countries. More than half of the cross-country variation in income per capita—and even more so in the variation of the growth rate of income per capita—arises from differences in TFP levels. Why do TFP levels differ so much, and why do they grow at different rates in different countries?

I argued in Chapters 4 and 5 that investment in research and development explains a substantial part of this variation, particularly in the industrial countries. An industrial country benefits directly from its own R&D and indirectly from the R&D efforts of other industrial countries. In contrast, developing countries—which invest very little in R&D—gain mostly from the innovative activities of the industrial countries. The cumulative effort of all countries combined advances the world technology frontier, and this changes differentially the opportunities of countries at different stages of development, and thereby the speed of their TFP growth. Advanced countries have to innovate in order to push out the technology frontier; less-developed countries garner productivity gains by catching up to the frontier.[1]

Substantial variation in growth remains, however, after accounting for both accumulation and R&D investment. The question is, Why?

Mokyr (2002) has described in great detail how the accumulation of knowledge transformed the Western countries into modern economies. This transformation could not have happened, however, without the formation of institutions that encouraged the accumulation of knowledge and its application to the development of new technologies. Not only did property rights need protection, but the modernization processes itself needed to be guarded against resistance from self-interested groups that stood to lose from it. In these circumstances political institutions have played an important role; they frame the struggle between the proponents of change and their opponents, and thereby affect the ability of countries to innovate and to implement new technologies.

Property rights secure the accumulation of capital, as Adam Smith argued long ago. This applies also to the accumulation of knowledge. Without the protection of property rights, capital formation, land development, and investment in R&D cannot take place. For this reason institutions that promote the rule of law, enforce contracts, and limit the power of rulers are important for economic development. These institutions protect individuals both from one another and from the state.[2] Djankov, Glaeser, and colleagues (2003) have argued that, because governments that can protect individuals from private infringement of property rights can themselves infringe on private property, institutional design embodies a fundamental conflict between the goal of controlling disorder and the goal of limiting the power of the executive—or, as they put it, a conflict between "disorder and dictatorship." This produces a tradeoff, which has important implications for the control of business: "We argue that the four common strategies of such control, namely private orderings, private litigation, regulation, and state ownership, can be viewed as points on the institutional possibility frontier, ranked in terms of increasing state powers" (6). In the tradeoff between disorder and dictatorship, institutions and politics are inseparable. Together they determine the ability of countries to accumulate, to innovate, to adopt new technologies, and to reorganize in the face of technological change. And they shape the economic policies that either promote or hinder growth.

## Historical Evolution

North (1981, 1990) examined the contribution of institutional developments to economic growth throughout history. In his view the Neolithic Revolution, ten thousand years ago, fundamentally altered the rate of human progress. Settled agriculture necessitated new organizational forms, because it required a system of property rights. These property rights were communal at the beginning, but they evolved over time, and the design of state and individual property rights played a particularly important role in shaping economic change. In time, political structures emerged, and the state became a fundamental player in the development of the ancient world. The state emerged with a body of rules that ordered its internal structure, and it maintained coercive power to enforce these rules. It also formalized property rights, which played a key role in the development of market institutions. During the Roman empire property rights were codified into Roman law.

The collapse of the Roman Empire had dire economic consequences. However, it represents just one major break in technological progress, organizational change, and economic growth in the West. Western history is replete with examples of the rise and fall of nations and empires, in both absolute and relative terms. The declines are particularly important, because they have been propelled by institutional and organizational failures. According to North (1981, 59), organizational success and failure account for the progress and retrogression of societies. Technological know-how is necessary for success, but it is not sufficient.

North (1981, 159–160) viewed the Industrial Revolution in a similar light, as a major institutional and organizational change. Although the West's acceleration in the rate of innovation preceded the traditional dates of the Industrial Revolution, it was better-specified property rights that improved the functioning of markets. And it was the rise in the size of the market that increased specialization, the division of labor, and the rate of return to innovation.[3] Transaction costs increased in this process, and organizational changes were devised to reduce them. These were indeed the developments that paved the way for an economic revolution in the second half of the nineteenth century, which consisted of the wedding of science and technology. This revolution generated critical knowledge that led to unprecedented developments in the Western world. They included rapid population growth, the attainment of a high standard of living, the decline of agriculture relative to manufacturing, large-scale urbanization, and continuous technological change as a norm.

North (1990) used a game analogy to illustrate the difference between institutions and organizations: institutions are the rules of the game, while organizations are the players. The players can consist of groups that are bound by a common interest, be it economic, social, political, or educational. The evolving role of these players is influenced by the rules that govern the game. But they, in turn, affect the evolution of the rules.[4]

According to Greif (n.d., chap. 2), North's definition of institutions is too narrow. He therefore proposes a broader, alternative definition, which encompasses North's as well as various other definitions commonly used by sociologists and political scientists: "an institution is a system of institutional elements that conjointly generate a regularity of behavior by enabling, guiding, and motivating it," where institutional elements are man-made nonphysical factors that are exogenous to each individual whose behavior they influence. Significantly, institutional elements include organizations.[5] One can therefore think about institutions as systems of rules, beliefs, and organizations. Rules coordinate behavior and enable people to act efficiently with few informational requirements. The beliefs are important for two reasons. First, even in institutions with formal structures people have to be motivated to follow the rules. And second, some institutions have informal structures, and they can be sustained only if people believe that actions will lead to well-defined rewards or punishments. People follow the rules and choose the expected actions because this is the best they can do within the prevailing institutional structure.

Greif emphasizes the importance of a context-specific analysis of institutions. The context-specific analysis is essential, because multiple equilibria are often possible in the formation of institutions in given circumstances—that is, more than one set of institutions can emerge in given circumstances. Examining the contextual details helps to clarify why particular institutions emerged in a particular historical setting and how they could be sustained, because historical path-dependence is an important element in the evolution of institutions.

Greif's analysis of the functioning of institutions is highly original, combining sophisticated game theory with detailed knowledge of history. Much of this work is summarized in his magnum opus, "Institutions: Theory and History" (n.d.). But his basic approach was illustrated in Greif (1993), where he studied the formation of a private institution by a network of Maghribi traders that operated around the Mediterranean in the eleventh century.[6] They were descendants of Jewish immigrants who fled the area around Baghdad for political reasons in the tenth century and settled in North Africa. They formed a close community with tightly held cultural beliefs and strong family ties. Some of them served as merchants and others as agents of merchants. Overseas agents provided the merchants with trade-related services, operating on their behalf at distant locations.

Records indicate that among the Maghribi traders the use of agents was the rule in commercial transactions.[7] But merchants were not able to monitor their distant agents directly. In addition, the legal system provided only limited redress, and most of the agency relations were not based on legal contracts. How were these relations sustained?

Using the historical evidence, Greif attributed the success of the Maghribi traders to an institution they developed that solved the commitment problem that is inherent in every agency relationship. The Maghribi traders formed a coalition consisting of merchants who were members of the community. They adopted a set of cultural rules of behavior—the Merchants' Law—that agents were expected to follow. Within the merchants' coalition information was rapidly disseminated. An agent who did not follow the rules was deemed to be dishonest, and the news of his dishonesty spread rapidly within the community. The result was that a dishonest agent was not rehired by the merchant whom he cheated, nor by any other member of the community, for a substantial period of time. This multilateral punishment strategy made cheating very costly, and especially so in view of the fact that the options of an agent outside the Maghribi community were significantly less attractive.[8] This example illustrates the emergence and functioning of institutions that support economic activity. It also demonstrates historical path-dependence, because the institution resulted from a political process that triggered the migration of its founders from Baghdad to North Africa.

Although the institution developed by the Maghribi traders enabled them to expand trade by means of agents, the scope of impersonal exchange—that is, exchange that does not rely on personal relationships—was limited in this arrangement and so was its geographical reach. However, the extension of impersonal exchange over large territories was key to the late medieval Commercial Revolution, which took place between the eleventh and the fourteenth centuries. Forming institutions of impersonal exchange was an important part of this revolution, which occurred at a time when legal systems were not well developed and the authority of courts was limited to local communities. Moreover, where courts existed, they were not impartial; they were controlled by the local elite (landed or urban) and they tended to discriminate against outsiders. Greif (n.d., chap. 8) has analyzed the emergence in this environment of the Community Responsibility System, a contract-enforcement mechanism that sustained impersonal transactions between members of different communities.

In the late medieval period many European communities had well-defined memberships and were self-governed. As a result it was possible to recognize the community affiliation of parties to a transaction. According to the rules of the Community Responsibility System, the entire community was responsible for the deeds of each one of its members. This meant that if a party to a transaction from one community cheated a member of another community, all members of the offender's community were liable for his misconduct. The practical implication was that every member of the offender's community could be called upon to pay for the damage caused by the offender. If a member of the offender's community happened to be in the jurisdiction of the community of the person who had been cheated, the member of the offender's community could be sued in the local court and the property in his immediate possession, such as merchandise, could be confiscated. Under the circumstances a community had strong incentives to ensure that each one of its members was in good standing in other communities. Every local community therefore enforced the commitments of its members to residents of other communities.[9]

Greif has developed a repeated-game model in which a Community Responsibility System is an equilibrium outcome, and he provides anecdotal evidence from England and Florence in support of his model. He also argues that the organizational structure of Champagne's great medieval fairs took advantage of the Community Responsibility System.

Improvements in the organization of trade, or more generally in the organization of economic activities, are every bit as important as improvements in technology. If we had data that allowed us to calculate TFP growth during the medieval period, we probably would have found that the institutional innovations of the

Maghribi traders or the molders of the Community Responsibility System led to TFP growth. Such data are not available, however. As a result it is not possible to derive a quantitative assessment of the contribution of these institutional developments to economic growth. Nevertheless, since—as we saw in Chapter 5—market integration is important for growth, an analysis of nonmarket institutions and their relation to market integration should lead to a better understanding of the growth process.

## Legal Origins

Legal systems play a central role in the protection of property rights. They differ, however, across countries, and these differences affect the functioning of national economies. Glaeser and Shleifer (2002) studied the evolution of the English common-law and the French civil-law systems, which are the most prevalent systems worldwide. They noted that "civil law relies on professional judges, legal codes, and written records, while common law relies on lay judges, broader legal principles, and oral arguments" (1193). And they suggested that the stronger the pressure on courts to rule in favor of powerful litigants, the greater the need for centralization of the legal system. But although greater centralization can reduce disorder, it gives the center more power. Moreover, in orderly environments with central control a decentralized legal system is easier to enforce, while in disorderly environments with weak central control a central legal system is easier to enforce. As a result, France—which was relatively disorderly in the twelfth and the thirteenth centuries, and had a weak central government—adopted the civil-law system, which gives greater power to the center. But England—which was relatively peaceful in the twelfth and thirteenth centuries and had strong central control—adopted the common-law system, which is more decentralized. That is, France chose to rely on state-employed judges precisely because local lords were powerful while England chose a jury system because its local lords were weak. And these differences in local conditions persisted for centuries.

Through colonization, the civil-law and common-law systems were transplanted to many countries, thereby molding their economic and political makeup. Detailed studies have examined the effects of these legal systems on the protection of investor rights, the regulation of business activity, the regulation of labor, and the quality of government. La Porta and colleagues (1998) showed that the quality of present-day laws that protect investor rights and the quality of their enforcement vary by the origin of the legal system in a sample of forty-nine countries: they are strongest in common-law countries, weakest in French civil-law countries, and in between in Scandinavian and German civil-law countries. And La Porta and colleagues (1999) showed that countries with a common-law system have better governments—as measured by indexes of property rights protection, the quality of business regulation, and the top marginal tax rate—than countries with a French civil-law system.

Djankov, La Porta, and colleagues (2003) studied the efficiency of courts in resolving disputes in 109 countries. They used two legal procedures as measures of efficiency: the eviction of a nonpaying tenant and the collection of a bounced check. From detailed information about these procedures they constructed a measure of procedural formalism for each one of the countries. And they found that legal origin explains 40 percent of the cross-country variation in procedural formalism, which is higher in French civil-law countries than in English common-law countries. Using OLS regressions, they found that higher procedural formalism leads to longer duration of dispute resolution for both eviction and check collection, lower enforceability of contracts, and higher corruption.[10] The results did not change when they estimated these relationships with instrumental variables, using legal origin as an instrument for procedural formalism.

In another study, Djankov and colleagues (2002) examined the regulation of entry in eighty-five countries, using explicit measures of difficulty in forming a new firm, such as the number of procedures required to start up a firm and the number of days it takes to execute these procedures. They found wide variation in these measures across countries, as well as wide variation in their official cost, which was as low as 0.5 percent of GDP per capita in the United States and as high as 460 percent of GDP per capita in the Dominican Republic. And these costs differed by legal origin. French and German civil-law countries, as well as countries with socialist legal origin, had more regulation than English common-law countries, while Scandinavian civil-law countries had regulation comparable to that of English common-law countries. Evidently these entry costs impose a burden on business firms and limit competition, but the study found that stricter regulation is also associated with higher levels of corruption and larger shares of unofficial economic activity.[11]

Summarizing the findings on the regulation of courts, entry, and labor markets,[12] Djankov, Glaeser, and colleagues (2003) noted that "in all three areas, i.e., entry, courts, and labor markets, socialist and French legal origin countries regulate much more heavily than do the common law countries. On average, the same countries that regulate entry, also regulate courts and labor markets; these correlations are at least partly driven by legal origin" (24).

## Colonial Origins

The influence of institutions imposed by colonizing powers on the development of various territories and countries has received particular attention. Some have argued that a colonizer has a decisive impact on the formation of its former colony's political, legal, and economic institutions, and thereby on the former colony's economic performance.[13] North, Summerhill, and Weingast (2000) furnished particularly strong arguments along this line, contrasting the development of North with South America. They argued that differences in the governing structure of the Spanish and British empires, and their divergent needs during the colonial era, explain to a large extent why political institutions which fostered order—and were conducive to economic development—formed in North America under British rule, but very different institutions—which bred disorder and were not conducive to economic development—emerged in Latin America under Spanish rule.[14] Although North, Summerhill, and Weingast did not deny that resource and other factor endowments affected the formation of institutions, as argued by Coatsworth (1993) and Engerman and Sokoloff (1997), they insisted that the colonizer played a decisive role.

According to Engerman and Sokoloff (1997) and Sokoloff and Engerman (2000), resource and other factor endowments determined specialization patterns in the colonies. They also determined the regional allocation of the six million immigrants to the New World during the sixteenth, seventeenth, and eighteenth centuries, of whom more than 60 percent were African slaves. The areas that most attracted migrants who had a choice in the matter had soil and climate that were suitable for the production of lucrative commodities such as sugar and coffee; they included the West Indies and parts of South America. The production of these crops was organized in large plantations with slave labor, creating large inequalities in wealth and political power. These characteristics in turn fostered the formation of economic and political institutions that favored the plantation owners, thereby propagating inequality and hampering economic development.

In other parts of Spanish America, the factor endowments were characterized by rich mineral resources and substantial numbers of natives who could be employed in their extraction. There the Spanish authorities distributed grants of land to favorites of the crown, again producing large inequalities of wealth and political power, which shaped the evolution of extractive institutions that were not conducive to growth.

In contrast, the northern part of North America had few native inhabitants and the soil was suitable for grains rather than for the lucrative crops of the West Indies. As a result, large plantations did not spring up and most of the laborers were of European descent. These conditions created much less inequality of wealth and political power, which encouraged the shaping of more egalitarian institutions and better protection of individual property rights. These in turn provided investment incentives to large segments of society and thereby promoted growth.

Sokoloff and Engerman (2000) argued, however, that the roles of the British and Spanish crowns could not be as starkly different as suggested by North, Summerhill, and Weingast (2000). They pointed out that during the colonial period the economies with the highest per capita income were in the Caribbean, and among them no marked difference existed between those that were Spanish, British, or French. This implies that endowments were more important than colonizers. More generally, colonies that belonged to the same empire—British or Spanish—varied in their level of economic success, and this variation was in large measure due to factor endowments.

Acemoglu, Johnson, and Robinson (2001, 2002) have provided the strongest evidence for the argument that local conditions rather than the identity of the colonizing power determined institutional development and economic growth. Their theory consists of three building blocks. First, the European colonizers could choose from a range of strategies; at one extreme, they could form extractive institutions without European settlement in the colonies, and at the other, they could settle in the colonies and replicate their institutions there. Second, the choice of strategy was influenced by local conditions. In particular, the extractive strategy was followed when the conditions for settlement were not favorable. And third, once the institutions were formed, they persisted after independence.

To test this theory, Acemoglu, Johnson, and Robinson (2001) collected data on mortality rates in the colonies between the seventeenth and nineteenth centuries of European bishops, sailors, and soldiers who did not die in battle. The mortality rate was treated as a proxy for the degree of difficulty of settling in an area; the higher the mortality rate the more difficult it must have been to settle there. Acemoglu, Johnson, and Robinson showed that the mortality rate is negatively correlated with GDP per capita in 1995, meaning that income per capita in 1995 was high in areas that were hospitable to European settlers more than a hundred years earlier and low in areas that were not. Moreover, these authors showed that the mortality rate is positively correlated with an index of expropriation risk during 1985–1995.[15] If we interpret low expropriation risk as a reflection of good institutions, this second correlation implies that areas that were hospitable to European settlers in the seventeenth, eighteenth or nineteenth centuries ended up with good institutions at the end of the twentieth century, and those that were not hospitable to European settlers ended up with bad institutions.

But do these two correlations necessarily imply that the local conditions in the colonies, between the seventeenth and the nineteenth centuries, affected income per capita in 1995 through the shaping of institutions? Or do they result from other sources of variation? Acemoglu, Johnson, and Robinson employed the two-stage least-squares method to estimate the impact of institutions on GDP per capita, using settler mortality rates as instruments. They estimated a first-stage equation in which the measure of expropriation risk was regressed on settler mortality rates, and a second-stage equation in which GDP per capita was regressed on the measure of expropriation risk. They found the estimated coefficients to be highly significant. Settler mortality had a significant impact on expropriation risk and expropriation risk had a significant impact on GDP per capita.[16] A sensitivity analysis confirmed the robustness of these findings.

Did the colonial origin of a country affect only the quality of its institutions, or did it also have a direct impact on its income per capita? In the sensitivity analysis the finding was that it did both. At the same time, however, controlling for the colonial origin does not diminish the influence of the settler mortality rate, a finding that supports the claim that variations in local conditions played an independent role in the emergence of institutions and in their impact on long-term development.

Of particular interest are the legal systems that were transplanted by the colonizers to the colonies, because (as discussed in the previous section) legal systems have systematic effects on the protection of property rights and the quality of governmental institutions. Acemoglu, Johnson, and Robinson confirmed these results. In their sample of sixty-four countries the legal system is either of English common-law origin or of French civil-law origin. They found that the English common-law system had a better effect on the formation of institutions (for example, it produced lower expropriation risk). Controlling for legal origin, however, did not much change the estimated impact of local conditions on institutions and through them on GDP per capita in 1995. This result corroborates the important effects that local conditions had in the colonies on the formation of institutions and through them on prosperity at the end of the twentieth century.

Acemoglu and Johnson (2003) went one step further in separating the effects of property rights from contracting institutions. Using the risk of government expropriation and constraints on the executive as proxies of the property rights institutions, and measures of legal formalisms from Djankov, La Porta, and colleagues (2002, 2003) as proxies of contracting institutions, they examined the effects of these institutions on the long-run growth of a sample of countries that are former European colonies. In order to deal with the endogeneity problems of these institutional measures, they instrumented the contracting institutions with legal origin and the property rights institutions with settler mortality rates. And they found strong support for the importance of property rights institutions in fostering economic growth. That is, countries with stronger protection of property rights and greater constraints on the executive have higher income per capita. Once the effects of the property rights are controlled for, however, contracting institutions do not appear to affect income per capita. The researchers interpret this result as suggesting that countries cannot function well without protection of property rights, but that the private sector can structure its transactions—such as the financing of economic activity—in ways that overcome the deficiencies of the contracting institutions. Although this analysis provides an important step in the direction of identifying separate institutional channels of influence, the robustness of the conclusion awaits further scrutiny.

## Geography versus Institutions

Some authors argue that institutions play a primary role in economic development, while others assign this role to geography. Sachs (2001) in particular has defended the view that geography plays a major role in the economic success of countries. He has argued that regions that are temperate or have access to sea-based trade have a considerable advantage over regions that are tropical or land-locked. Using a climate classification system that differentiates regions by temperature and precipitation, he examined regional patterns of growth and development. Temperate zones and coastal regions had higher income per capita. Moreover, using Maddison's (1995) historical data he found that between 1820 and 1992 temperate regions grew at an average rate of 1.4 percent per capita while nontemperate zones grew only at 0.9 percent. In addition, following Barro (1991), he regressed the average annual growth rate of income per capita between 1965 and 1990 on initial income per capita and education, as well as on the share of a country's population living in a temperate zone. He found that the share of a country's population living in a temperate zone had a positive effect on its growth rate.[17]

The dispute about geography versus institutions is not so much about whether geography affects economic development, however, as about whether it affects development through the formation of institutions or via other channels. Hall and Jones (1999), who found large productivity differences across countries, thought that development occurred through institutions: "[Our] central hypothesis . . . is that the primary, fundamental determinant of a country's long-run economic performance is its social infrastructure. By social infrastructure we mean the institutions and government policies that provide the incentives for individuals and firms in an economy" (95). Those incentives can encourage innovation and accumulation, or they can encourage rent-seeking, corruption, and theft.

To support this position, Hall and Jones estimated the impact of institutions on output per worker by means of the two-stage least-squares method, using various measures of western European influence as instruments for institutions. Among these instruments they included a geographic characteristic, the distance from the equator.[18]

Sachs (2001) criticized the validity of this instrument, arguing that latitude is a poor measure of the degree of penetration of European institutions, because many midlatitude regions, such as Central Asia, China, Korea, and Japan, have in fact weak ties to Europe. On the other hand, many equatorial regions are former (or current) European colonies, with strong ties to Europe.

This criticism is well taken. Indeed, Acemoglu, Johnson, and Robinson (2001) found that adding latitude to their equations did not much change the relationship between institutions and

GDP per capita, and that the effects of latitude either were not significant or were even of the wrong sign.

Economic outcomes hardly ever have a single cause, and this applies with particular force to the complex process of long-run development. For this reason the debate about institutions versus geography is better framed as a debate about the *relative* importance of these attributes as determinants of income and wealth. Although the quantitative estimates of the contribution to income per capita of institutions relative to geography are not very reliable, a 2002 study by Acemoglu, Johnson, and Robinson tilts the balance strongly in favor of the primacy of institutions.

To begin with, Acemoglu, Johnson, and Robinson (2002) documented what they called "reversal of fortune." That is, they found that countries or territories that were relatively rich around 1500 had become relatively poor by 1995; and vice versa, countries and territories that were relatively poor around 1500 had become relatively rich by 1995. They used two measures of well-being in 1500: urbanization, measured by the fraction of people living in towns with more than five thousand inhabitants, and population density, measured by the number of people per unit area. Both measures are believed to be highly correlated with living standards.[19] Figure 7.1 depicts the remarkable relationship between population density in 1500 and GDP per capita in 1995 (adjusted for purchasing power parity) for a sample of ninety-two countries. Every point in the figure represents a country.[20] The figure shows a negative correlation between living standards in 1500 and living standards in 1995. The authors then showed convincingly that geography-based hypotheses cannot explain this pattern, while an institution-based hypothesis can.

First, this sort of data obviously rejects a simple static view of

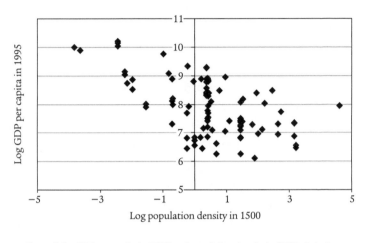

**Figure 7.1**  GDP per capita in 1995 and population density in 1500. Data from Acemoglu, Johnson, and Robinson (2002).

the effects of geography on development, because if geographic attributes dominated development, then regions that were rich at the beginning of the sixteenth century should also have been rich at the end of the twentieth century. Second, one could argue, as Sachs (2001) did, that areas that were prosperous at the beginning of the sixteenth century had soil and climate that were suitable for the agricultural technologies of the time, but they lost this advantage when new agricultural technologies developed that favored temperate areas. But this explanation was rejected by Acemoglu, Johnson, and Robinson, who showed that the reversal in the relative ranking of countries took place sometime between the end of the eighteenth century and the beginning of the nineteenth. The reversal thus did not take place during the period of major technological progress in agriculture, but rather much later, during the Industrial Revolution, and it was related to industrialization.

Acemoglu, Johnson, and Robinson (2002) suggested instead that the reversal of fortune can be explained by the institutions that were formed by the European colonizers. On the one hand, relatively poor regions were sparsely populated, which made them attractive to European settlers. Once the Europeans settled in a region in large numbers, they had an incentive to establish institutions that provided for themselves broad protection of property rights and broadly distributed political power.[21] In prosperous, densely populated areas, on the other hand, settlement was less attractive to Europeans. In these areas it was more attractive to form extractive institutions, based on both economic and political inequality.[22] When the Industrial Revolution came along, the former type of institutions furthered it, while the latter type deterred it.

Econometric evidence suggests that prosperity in the early part of the sixteenth century is correlated both with bad institutions in the late part of the twentieth century, as measured by an index of expropriation risk, and with bad institutions in the first year of independence, as measured by an index of constraint on the executive. These correlations persist after controlling for latitude. Again using two-stage least squares, Acemoglu, Johnson, and Robinson (2002) estimated the impact of institutions on per capita income in 1995, using settler mortality in the seventeenth, eighteenth, and nineteenth centuries and prosperity circa 1500 as instruments. They found that institutions that were formed centuries earlier had a significant impact on well-being at the end of the twentieth century. Moreover, they could not reject the hypothesis that prosperity at the beginning of the sixteenth century had no independent effect on the twentieth-century level of well-being, except for its impact through the formation of institutions. That is, the conditions at the beginning of the sixteenth century affected well-being in the twentieth century primarily through their impact on institutional design. Finally, using the industrial output of the UK as a measure of industrialization, they found that the interaction of institutions with industrialization had a positive effect on a country's well-being. Countries with good institutions took better advantage of industrialization than countries with bad institutions.[23]

More recent econometric studies by Easterly and Levine (2003) and Rodrik, Subramanian, and Trebbi (2002) confirmed the key finding of Acemoglu, Johnson, and Robinson regarding the primacy of institutions as compared with geography in the long-run determination of income per capita.[24] Although geographical characteristics may have influenced the formation of institutions and thereby long-term development, the geographical traits of a country have no direct impact on its income per capita once the effects of institutions are accounted for.[25]

## Political Economy

Economic and political interests interact in shaping economic development. The question is, How? Przeworski and colleagues (2000, chap. 3) argued, for example, that democratic regimes do not grow at different rates than autocratic regimes, while Mulligan and Sala-i-Martin (2003) argued that there are no systematic economic and social policy differences between democratic and (noncommunist) nondemocratic regimes.[26] Yet real wages are higher in democracies.[27] And higher income per capita brackets have higher fractions of countries with democratic regimes.[28]

Huntington (1968) emphasized the role of stability in the survival of regimes. But change per se does not appear to be harmful to regimes. Rather, change that results from economic growth is good for the survival of both democratic and autocratic regimes, while contraction of income per capita is detrimental to the survival of both.[29] Investment rates are higher in nondemocratic regimes, but this is predominantly the result of low levels of income per capita in these countries. As explained in Chapter 2, we should expect higher investment rates in poorer countries, and the evidence supports this relationship. And indeed, once differences in income per capita are accounted for, democracies do not appear to have lower investment rates.[30]

Modernization theory argues that economic development leads to the democratization of autocratic regimes. As a country becomes richer, its social structure becomes more complex, new groups emerge with their own needs and power, and it becomes more difficult to sustain an autocratic regime. According to Lipset (1959), the cumulative process of industrialization, urbanization, rising education levels, and political mobilization leads in the end to democratization. The evidence on the Lipset hypothesis, however, is mixed for the postwar period. On the one hand, Barro (1997, chap. 2) estimated a positive impact of GDP per capita on democracy and civil liberties, which supports the hypothesis. On the other hand, Przeworski and colleagues (2000, chap. 2) found that higher income does not raise the probability of a switch from autocracy to democracy, but rather that democracies are more likely to survive in higher-income countries.[31] This higher survival probability explains the positive correlation between the fraction of democratic regimes and income per capita in these authors' data. And this may also explain the positive correlation between income per capita and democracy in Barro's data set. If so, the data do not support the Lipset hypothesis.[32]

Acemoglu and Robinson (2003) offered a theory of transition from dictatorship to democracy that uses the redistributive conflict between the rich and the poor as the main driving force behind political change. In their theory, social and political groups are interested not only in current redistributive policies but also in future policies. A group can secure advantageous policies in the future by promoting the formation of institutions that give it political power. The numerous poor have more political power in a democracy; the fewer rich have more political power in an autocracy. But political power can be formal or based on brute force. When the poor in a nondemocratic regime attain political power, possibly by force and only temporarily, they press for a transition to democracy, which gives them formal political power. The new regime provides a commitment device for future pro-poor policies.

According to this theory a revolution is more attractive to the poor the larger the inequality. But larger inequality makes democracy more costly to the rich and makes repression more attractive to them. As a result of these opposing influences, the theory predicts an inverted U-shaped relationship between inequality and the likelihood of democratization. Democratization is unlikely when inequality is small or large, and it is most likely at intermediate levels of inequality.[33]

Conflicts over redistribution play out in many forms in the political arena. The links between economics and politics do not concern the poor and the rich only, because groups organize along varying dimensions in order to protect their interests. Excellent examples are provided by Rogowski's (1989) analysis of the effects of international trade on political alignments.

Rogowski used the Stolper-Samuelson theorem to analyze how the interests of labor, land owners, and capital owners shifted in response to changing conditions in the world economy.[34] In a Heckscher-Ohlin analytical framework, this theorem suggests that improved conditions on world markets, which may result from falling trade costs or reduced foreign protection, benefit inputs that are abundant in a country, because they are used intensively in the production of exportable products. Inputs that are used intensively in the production of import-competing products lose.

Rogowski examined the effects of the first wave of globalization in the last part of the nineteenth century on the formation of political coalitions. Contrasting Britain, Germany, and the United States, he noted that both Germany and the United States were capital-poor at the time in comparison with Britain. But while Germany was rich in labor and poor in land, the United States was rich in land and poor in labor. The expansion of trade, therefore, benefited labor in Germany and threatened the income of capital and land there. As a result, labor supported free trade while capital and land formed the infamous "marriage of iron and rye" to oppose free trade. In the United States, labor and capital united into a protectionist coalition, while landowners favored free trade. The result was rural-urban conflict. Finally, in Britain, which was rich in capital and labor, a coalition of capital and labor supported free trade while landowners supported protection.[35]

These are examples of the impact of economic conditions on politics. The causality can go the other way as well. Consider the political economy of trade protection. Grossman and Helpman (1994b) proposed a model of protection in which economic interests organize along sectoral lines, so that interest groups form to represent industries. Their model predicts a cross-sectional structure of protection that depends on political and economic characteristics. In particular, the average level of protection depends both on how much weight policy makers attach to aggregate welfare as opposed to political support in the form of contributions and on what fraction of people are represented by active interest groups.[36] A number of empirical studies estimated the model's parameters with data from various countries.[37] Mitra, Thomakos, and Ulubaşoğlu (2002) estimated it for Turkey, both for the period of military rule and for the later period following democratization. They found that the switch from military rule to democracy raised the relative weight of aggregate welfare and the fraction of people represented by interest groups, which in turn reduced the level of protection.

These examples of links between economics and politics in the realm of international trade illustrate the importance of political economy. But they do not shed light on *how* political economy affects growth, because (as we saw in Chapter 5) there are no simple links between growth and levels of protection. For this reason we also cannot expect to find simple links between political economy and rates of growth. Yet such links can and should be studied, because they hold the key to some of the mysteries of economic growth.[38]

Olson (1982) advanced a hypothesis that directly links the formation of political factions to growth. Starting with *The Logic of Collective Action* (1965), Olson suggested that the formation of interest groups does not further economic efficiency. Moreover, stable societies tend to accumulate more groups that promote their own interests. The activities of these groups then reduce efficiency and foster political divisiveness. Despite the fact that large organizations weigh the loss of aggregate efficiency against their own distributional gains, significant excess burden emerges in societies with such organized groups. They slow down the social process of decision making, erect entry barriers, produce complex legal and regulatory frameworks, and complicate the role of government. As a result they damage a society's capacity to adopt new technologies and to reorganize in response to technological change. Thus they slow growth.[39] In short, in stable societies the number of groups that seek redistributive gains grows over time and the rate of growth of income per capita declines.

Discussing the post–World War II experience, Olson (1982) argued that "countries that have had democratic freedom of organization without upheaval or invasion the longest will suffer the most from growth-repressing organizations" (77). For this reason, totalitarianism, instability, and war destroyed special-interest groups in Germany, Japan, and France. Stability and the lack of invasion allowed such groups to flourish, however, in the United Kingdom. As a result, Olson argued, Germany and Japan—whose economies were devastated by the war—experienced an "economic miracle" in the postwar period; France—which was only occupied—did not experience a "miracle" but grew at a considerably fast rate; and the UK—which was not invaded—performed poorly. And the same argument explains why Switzerland, a country that did not participate in the war, grew even more slowly than the UK.[40]

Olson's view has been challenged, however. First, Booth, Melling, and Dartmann (1997) showed that many of the special-interest organizations that existed in Germany before the war reappeared there after the war. In other words, the war did not abolish some of the main organizations that Olson deemed detrimental to Germany's success. Second, there is no evidence in the Przeworski and colleagues (2000, chap. 4) data that the rate of growth declines with the age of a regime, democratic or autocratic, and Persson and Tabellini (2003, chap. 7) found that older democracies pursue policies that are more favorable to growth. Evidently the effects of interest groups are more subtle than Olson's theory suggests. Yet we still do not have a combined theory of growth and interest-group formation and dismantling. We obviously need such a theory in order to better understand the mechanisms through which interest groups affect economic growth and how they reorganize in the face of economic change.[41]

We also do not have a good theory that links political institutions to growth, nor have we reliable empirical evidence on these links. Nevertheless, progress is being made. Persson and Tabellini (2003) provided a detailed study of the effects of electoral rules and the form of government on economic outcomes. They collected a large data set for the postwar period that enabled them to estimate the impact of presidential and parliamentary forms of government, and majoritarian and proportional electoral rules, on government spending, taxation, and other policies that affect productivity and growth.[42] They found that the effects of the form of government interact in subtle ways with democratic institutions. In good and well-established democracies, economic policies are more growth oriented in presidential than in parliamentary regimes. In weak democracies, the opposite is true: economic policies are more growth oriented in parliamentary regimes. Persson and Tabellini also found that older democracies pursue policies that are more favorable to growth than younger democracies, and that the older democracies are more productive as a result. And they found no significant difference between the effects of the two electoral rules on productivity and growth. Nevertheless, once the crude distinction between the electoral rules is abandoned, various details appear to exert important effects. In particular, in majoritarian systems small districts are detrimental to economic development.[43]

Persson (2003) reconsidered some of these findings in a larger sample of countries that includes nondemocratic regimes.

Using, for the democratic regimes, their age and constitutional type (parliamentary versus presidential) as instruments of anti-diversion policies,[44] in addition to the population share speaking one of the five primary European languages and the Frankel and Romer (1999) predicted trade share, he found in the cross section that age and constitutional type have a significant impact on labor productivity. Once the impact of these two variables on policies is controlled for, however, they have no further effect on labor productivity. Namely, the age of democratic regimes and their constitutional type affect labor productivity through the policy-formation process only. These effects are very large; the replacement of any regime with a parliamentary democracy improves a country's structural policies so as to raise its long-run labor productivity by 40 percent. Although these results are rather preliminary, they show how important it is to understand the effects of political institutions on economic performance. And they also prove that it is possible to study these complex issues.[45]

Countries that start with similar endowments can follow different developmental paths as a result of differences in institutional structures, because institutions affect the incentives to innovate and to develop new technologies, the incentives to reorganize production and distribution in order to exploit new opportunities, and the incentives to accumulate physical and human capital. For these reasons institutions are more fundamental determinants of economic growth than R&D or capital accumulation, human or physical. Yet economic studies of the impact of institutions on economic growth are very recent, despite the fact that economic historians and other social scientists have examined institutions for a long time. As a result, some important issues that I have discussed have not been satisfactorily resolved and the conclusions from this chapter are only tentative.

Major technological developments have taken place in countries that protected private property from infringement by individuals and the state. A legal system that facilitates transactions and a political system that constrains the executive are needed for this purpose. But these institutions are not sufficient for growth. The reason is that major changes in technology always induce major changes in economic organizations. The centralized factory in the late eighteenth century, the large business corporation in the late nineteenth century, the process of vertical integration at the beginning of the twentieth century, and the recent trend toward greater fragmentation of production exemplify organizational responses to technological change.[46] As a result, the ability of a country to grow also depends on its ability to accommodate such changes, and the ability to accommodate change depends in turn on a country's economic and political institutions.

The institutions that are good for one period are not necessarily good for another. Britain declined in the late nineteenth century not least because it did not adapt fast enough to the emerging technologies of that era. And the economic and political institutions that supported the post–World War II growth spurt in Japan and the new industrial countries of the Pacific Rim have proved to be inadequate more recently. Institutions too have to change in order to promote growth. In particular, they need to evolve in tandem with technology. But this happens rarely, because institutions evolve slowly. The mismatch between institutions and technology is particularly severe during periods of rapid technological change, and especially when drastic innovations of the GPT type take place.

Although it has been established that property rights institutions, the rule of law, and constraints on the executive are important for growth, the exact ways in which they affect income per capita are not well understood. And the roles played by a host of other economic and political institutions, such as the structure of labor relations and the regulation of interest groups, are even less well understood. Yet an understanding of these features of modern societies is extremely important for greater insight into modern economic growth. Without it, it is difficult to pinpoint reforms that can help achieve faster growth in both developed and developing countries.

To make progress on this front, future research has to identify the channels through which institutions affect growth and the ways in which various institutions interact. To illustrate, consider the finding in Persson and Tabellini (2003) that presidential systems are better for growth than parliamentary systems in countries with sound and long-established democratic traditions, but parliamentary systems perform better in weak democracies. What are the key channels through which the two regimes affect economic outcomes? Is it through tax policies? Restrictions on special interests? Responsiveness to change? Persson and Tabellini also discuss interactions between government forms and electoral systems, without clear conclusions. Yet these interactions may be significant. And the form of government may also interact in important ways with the legal system, labor market institutions, or the institutions that govern international trade and investment. The difficulty of identifying these separate influences multiplies as a result of the fact that when institutions evolve, their components—such as the legal and political systems—do not evolve independently of each other.

The study of institutions and their relation to economic growth is an enormous task on which only limited progress has been made so far. Nevertheless, renewed interest in this subject has produced new theoretical and empirical methods, new data sets, and new insights. We are now therefore better equipped to face this task.

GLOSSARY

NOTES

REFERENCES

INDEX

# GLOSSARY

**Capital intensity**  Ratio of capital to labor.

**Cobb-Douglas production function**  See *Production function.*

**Coefficient of variation**  A statistical measure of relative dispersion, defined as the ratio of the standard deviation of a distribution to its mean.

**Concave function**  A function in one variable $f(x)$ is concave when a given increase in $x$ raises $f(x)$ by less the larger $x$ is. This definition can be generalized to multivariable functions.

**Convergence**  Convergence in income per capita occurs when poor countries grow faster than rich countries. It is customary to say that there is *unconditional convergence* when in a cross section of countries the rate of growth of income per capita is negatively correlated with the initial level of income per capita. And it is customary to say that there is *conditional convergence* when this correlation exists after deducting from each country's growth rate the impact of variables that affect its steady state.

**Cross-section data**  A data set representing variations in a population at a point in time.

**Decile**  One of ten segments in a distribution, where every segment consists of adjacent points and every decile is of equal weight. These segments are ranked from low to high, so that the first decile contains the lowest points in the distribution while the tenth decile contains the highest points.

**Divergence**  Divergence in income per capita occurs when poor countries grow more slowly than rich countries.

**Endogeneity problem**  The simplest method of estimation used in economics, ordinary least squares (OLS) (see *Ordinary least squares*), provides unbiased estimates when various assumptions are satisfied. One of these assumptions is that when we estimate the impact of a variable $X$ on a variable $Y$, variable $X$ is exogenous. When variable $X$ is not exogenous, we have an endogeneity problem, in the sense that OLS yields a biased estimate. To correct this problem, two-stage least squares (see *Two-stage least squares*) are often used, with a suitable instrument (see *Instrument*) for $X$.

**Elasticity**  The elasticity of a variable $Y$ with respect to a variable $X$ measures the degree of responsiveness of $Y$ to changes in $X$. It is defined as the percentage increase in $Y$ that is caused by a 1 percent increase in $X$. The elasticity of substitution between two inputs $K$ and $L$ is defined as the percentage rise in the ratio $K/L$ when the relative cost of $K$ falls by 1 percent.

**Externality** An economic externality refers to the direct impact of one variable on another variable that does not take place through a market transaction. Pollution is a good example of a negative externality. When a power plant pollutes the environment, people living close to the plant suffer from the pollution. Another example is learning. When highly skilled workers from different companies in Silicon Valley meet in social circumstances and discuss recent technological advances, they learn from one another, imposing on each other a positive externality.

**Factor content** The factor content of a good measures the quantity of each input that was used to produce that good.

**Factor proportions theory of international trade** A trade theory that uses differences in factor endowments across countries to explain the structure of foreign trade. It is also referred to as the Heckscher-Ohlin trade theory, because Eli Heckscher and Bertil Ohlin were its founders.

**Fixed effects** When estimating the impact of certain variables $X_1, X_2, \ldots, X_n$ on a variable $Y$, using data that varies across countries and across time (see *Panel data*), it is often useful to introduce a variable that is specific to each country but does not vary over time, or a variable that is specific to every year but does not vary across countries. These variables account for unobserved country-specific (fixed) effects and unobserved time-specific (fixed) effects, respectively.

**Game** A strategic form of interaction that is often used to describe the interactions between individuals or business firms. An example would be two firms that compete in a market in which they are the sole suppliers. The strategy of each firm may be to set the price it charges for its product. A solution to the game is characterized by two prices, each one charged by one of the firms, such that no firm has an incentive to deviate from its price. When a game is played many times it is called a repeated game.

**General purpose technology (GPT)**   A technology with broad applications and pervasive use, such as electricity or the microprocessor.

**Geometric mean**   The (unweighted) geometric mean of positive variables $X_1, X_2, \ldots, X_n$ is given by their product raised to the power $1/n$.

**Gini coefficient**   A measure of income inequality. It is based on the Lorenz curve, which plots the relationship between the bottom fraction of individuals in the income distribution and the fraction of the total income that they earn, varying the bottom fraction of individuals between zero and one. An equal distribution of income is represented by a 45° straight-line Lorenz curve. The Gini coefficient is defined as the ratio of the area between the Lorenz line of perfect equality and the Lorenz curve constructed from the data to the entire area under the Lorenz line of perfect equality.

**Gravity equation**   The simplest form of the gravity equation of international trade flows postulates that these flows are proportional to the product of the GDP levels of the trading countries. More sophisticated forms of the gravity equation specify determinants of the factor of proportionality, which typically include variables that measure trade frictions, such as transport costs.

**Heckscher-Ohlin trade theory**  See *Factor proportions theory of international trade.*

**Hicks-neutral technical change**  Change in production efficiency that raises output by the same factor of proportionality for all combinations of inputs.

**Instrument**  When there is an endogeneity problem (see *Endogeneity problem*), in the sense that the variable $X$ whose impact on a variable $Y$ we seek to estimate is not exogenous, we can estimate the impact of $X$ on $Y$ if we can find a suitable instrument for $X$. A suitable instrument for $X$ is an exogenous variable $Z$ that is correlated with $X$ but not correlated with the residual in the relationship between $Y$ and $X$. If an instrument like this is available, the two-stage least squares method (see *Two-stage least squares*) can be used to estimate the impact of $X$ on $Y$.

**Log-linear approximation**  An approximation in the form of a Taylor expansion in which the variables are transformed into the natural logarithms of the original variables.

**Marginal product/productivity of capital**  The rise in output in response to a one-unit increase in the capital stock.

**Median**  The median of a distribution is the point at which half the mass of the distribution is below the point and half the mass is above it. A median voter is a voter whose most preferred outcome is such that half of the remaining voters prefer a lower outcome and the other half prefers a higher outcome.

**Neoclassical growth model**  Solow's growth model, including its extensions to multiple inputs and endogenous rates of saving.

**Ordinary least squares (OLS)** A statistical method for estimating the impacts of a set of variables $X_1, X_2, \ldots, X_n$ on a variable $Y$. The estimation method seeks parameters that minimize the sum of the squares of the deviations of Y from the predicted values.

**Panel data** A data set consisting of repeated cross sections (see *Cross-section data*) over time.

**Production function** A function that specifies the output levels that are obtained from different combinations of inputs. A Cobb-Douglas production function has a specific functional form, in which the output level equals the product of the inputs, each one raised to a fixed power. These power coefficients typically add up to one.

**Productivity** A measure of efficiency in a production relationship.

**Quintile** One of five segments in a distribution, where every segment consists of adjacent points and every quintile is of equal weight. These segments are ranked from low to high, so that the first quintile contains the lowest points in the distribution while the fifth quintile contains the highest points.

**Rate of return** The percentage return on an investment. If, for example, an investment of $100 returns after one year $105, then the annual rate of return is $(105 - 100)/100 = 0.05$; that is, the rate of return is 5 percent. The private rate of return measures the rate of return to a private investor. The social rate of return measures the rate of return to society.

**Rational expectations**  Expectations that are based on all the available information.

**R&D spillover**  The beneficial impact of R&D performed by one party on another party (see also *Externality*).

**Regression**  Regressing $Y$ on $X_1, X_2, \ldots, X_n$ means performing a procedure that estimates the individual impact of each variable $X_1, X_2, \ldots, X_n$ on $Y$.

**Returns to scale**  Returns to scale measure the impact of a proportional expansion of inputs on output. If a proportional expansion of inputs raises output by the rate of expansion of the inputs, we say that there are constant returns to scale. If the rate of expansion of output exceeds the rate of expansion of the inputs, there are increasing returns to scale. And if output expands at a lower rate, there are decreasing returns to scale.

**Spearman rank correlation coefficient**  A statistic that measures the strength of the ranking association between two variables. That is, it measures how close the ranking of the outcomes generated by one variable is to the ranking of the outcomes generated by the other variable.

**Terms of trade**  The ratio of an index of export prices to an index of import prices.

**Theil coefficient**  A measure of inequality, which can be either an income-weighted index or a population-weighted index. In the former case the index is calculated as the weighted average of the natural logarithms of the ratios of every group's income share to its population share, using income shares as weights. In the latter case the index is calculated as the weighted average of the natural logarithms of the ratios of every group's population share to its income share, using population shares as weights.

**Total factor productivity (TFP)**   A single measure of how efficiently all inputs combined are utilized in a production process.

**Transition probability**   The probability of switching from one state to another state.

**Two-stage least squares**   A method for estimating the impact of $X$ on $Y$ when there is an endogeneity problem (see *Endogeneity problem*). The method consists of estimating the impact of an instrument (see *Instrument*) $Z$ on $X$ in the first stage, and the estimation of the impact of the predicted value of $X$, from the first stage, on $Y$ in the second stage. When $Z$ satisfies the requirements of an instrument, the second-stage estimation provides an unbiased estimate of the impact of $X$ on $Y$.

# NOTES

## I. BACKGROUND

1. The United Nation's Human Development Index is a composite of measures of health, education, and income. It weights each one of these equally. The way in which the measure of income is constructed, however, causes it to rise less than proportionately with actual income.

2. According to Maddison (2001), in the year 1000, levels of real GDP per capita in Africa, Japan, and Asia exclusive of Japan were higher than in western Europe. But the differences were not very large; they were 4 percent, a little over 6 percent, and 12.5 percent, respectively. In contrast, in 1998 GDP per capita in western Europe was about thirteen times higher than in Africa and about six times higher than in Asia exclusive of Japan, while GDP per capita in Western offshoots (Australia, New Zealand, Canada, and the United States) was twenty times higher than in Africa and more than eight times higher than in Asia exclusive of Japan (see Maddison's table 3.1b).

3. See Durlauf and Quah (1999). They calculated transition probabilities from income per capita in year $t$ to income per capita in year $t+15$ for a sample of 105 countries over the period 1961 through

1988. The resulting dynamics exhibit a twin-peak property. The probability of a high-income country remaining a high-income country is high and the probability of a low-income country remaining a low-income country is also high. A middle-income country, however, has a higher probability of becoming a low-income or high-income country than of remaining a middle-income country. With this structure of transition probabilities the distribution converges over time to a bipolar mode: a group of rich countries and a group of poor countries. Jones (1997) reported in his figure 1 a shift in the distribution of GDP per worker across a large sample of countries from a single-peaked distribution in 1960 to a twin-peaked distribution in 1988. According to Jones, "there has been some convergence or 'catch-up' at the top of the income distribution and some divergence at the bottom" (22).

4. The source for Figure 1.1, Summers and Heston, PWT 5.6, refers to the Penn World Table, version 5.6, developed by Robert Summers and Alan Heston. See Summers and Heston (1991) for a description of an earlier version of these data.

5. The list of countries, arranged by continent, is: Algeria, Benin, Burkina Faso, Burundi, Cameroon, Cape Verde Islands, Central Africa Republic, Chad, Comoros, Congo, Egypt, Gabon, Gambia, Ghana, Guinea, Guinea-Biss, Ivory Coast, Kenya, Lesotho, Madagascar, Malawi, Mali, Mauritania, Mauritius, Morocco, Mozambique, Namibia, Nigeria, Rwanda, Senegal, Seychelles, South Africa, Togo, Tunisia, Uganda, Zambia, Zimbabwe; Canada, Costa Rica, Dominican Republic, El Salvador, Guatemala, Honduras, Jamaica, Mexico, Nicaragua, Panama, Trinidad and Tobago, United States; Argentina, Bolivia, Brazil, Chile, Colombia, Ecuador, Guyana, Paraguay, Peru, Uruguay, Venezuela; Bangladesh, China, Hong Kong, India, Indonesia, Iran, Israel, Japan, Jordan, Republic of Korea, Malaysia, Pakistan, Philippines, Singapore, Sri Lanka, Syria, Taiwan, Thailand; Austria, Belgium, Cyprus, Czechoslovakia, Denmark, Finland, France, West Germany, Greece, Iceland, Ireland, Italy, Luxembourg, Netherlands,

Norway, Portugal, Spain, Sweden, Switzerland, Turkey, United Kingdom, Yugoslavia; Australia, Fiji, New Zealand, Papua New Guinea.

6. The coefficient of variation is a statistical measure of dispersion. More dispersion is represented by a higher coefficient.

7. These 21 rich economies are part of the larger sample of 104 economies. They are: Canada, United States, Japan, Austria, Belgium, Denmark, Finland, France, West Germany, Greece, Ireland, Italy, Netherlands, Norway, Portugal, Spain, Sweden, Switzerland, United Kingdom, Australia, New Zealand.

8. The economic deterioration of these countries was caused for the most part by civil wars and the breakdown of civil institutions.

9. This acceleration in growth is the more remarkable in view of the fact that it transpired during a period of acceleration in population growth. Maddison (2001, table 1.2) reports that the rate of population growth increased from 0.17 percent in 1000–1820 to 0.98 percent in 1820–1998. Some economists have, in fact, argued that this demographic transition and the acceleration of economic growth are closely linked; see, for example, Becker, Murphy, and Tamura (1990) and Kremer (1993), and more recently Galor and Weil (2000), Galor and Moav (2002), and Lucas (2002, chap. 5).

## 2. ACCUMULATION

1. This means that all countries have the same technology, the same rate of capital depreciation, the same rate of technological progress, the same rate of population growth, and the same rate of saving. These assumptions are obviously too strong, and they have been relaxed in various applications. However, most applications maintain the assumption that at least some features of the technology and the rate of technological progress are common to all countries.

2. I use *income* and *output* interchangeably. This is a slight abuse of terms, except that income and output are the same in a world in which economies have no income from foreign sources. When the

difference between income and output is important, the distinction will be clearly stated.

3. It is assumed here that the number of workers is proportional to the population and every worker works a fixed number of hours. In this event, output per hour, not adjusted for productivity, changes at the same rate as output per capita.

4. An intersection of the two curves at a point such as E, at which the capital-labor ratio is larger than zero, is guaranteed when the marginal product of capital is high enough for low levels of capital intensity and declines fast enough as the capital intensity rises. When the first condition is not satisfied, saving always falls short of the required replacement, and capital intensity declines over time. On the other hand, when the first condition is satisfied but the second is not, saving always exceeds the required replacement. Under these circumstances capital intensity grows without bound and the long-run rate of growth of income per capita is positive even in the absence of technological progress. The situation depicted in Figure 2.1 is, however, the central case treated in this chapter.

5. Although the *growth rate* of income per capita does not depend on economic variables, such as the saving rate or the rate of population growth, the *level* of income per capita depends on these variables even in the long run. More on this below.

6. King and Rebelo used a modified version of Solow's model, which allows for endogenous savings that are optimized over time. The original version of this model is due to Cass (1965).

7. They did this by estimating an equation that is a log-linear approximation around the steady state of the true growth equation. Unlike Solow, Barro and Sala-i-Martin did not assume a constant rate of saving. Following Cass (1965) they assumed instead that consumers choose an optimal saving rate at every point in time. More important, when they estimated the rate of convergence, they controlled for cross-country differences in the long-run levels of capital intensity. But they imposed a common rate of convergence, despite the fact that the theoretical model implies that some of the variables

that influence long-run capital intensity also affect the rate of convergence. Under these circumstances the estimated rate of convergence should be interpreted as an average across countries. A similar approach was used by Mankiw, Romer, and Weil (1992) to estimate the rate of convergence, assuming a constant saving rate instead. They also found a rate of convergence close to 2 percent per annum.

8. Other studies, using panel data techniques, found faster rates of convergence. Islam (1995) estimated a rate of convergence of 6 percent per annum while Caselli, Esquivel, and Lefort (1996) estimated a rate of convergence of 10 percent. I believe that the higher estimates are more reliable, because the Barro and Sala-i-Martin (1992) estimates, as well as the estimates of Mankiw, Romer, and Weil (1992), suffer from a downward bias, for reasons discussed in the next chapter.

9. This statement disregards some nonmonotonic dynamics that can arise when one country has a higher stock of one type of capital (say, human) and a lower stock of the other type (say, physical). See Mulligan and Sala-i-Martin (1993).

10. Lane and Milesi-Ferretti (2001) reported that in the industrial countries the stock of foreign direct investment increased from about 2 percent of GDP in 1970 to more than 12 percent in 1998, and that foreign equity investment increased during that period from about 2 percent to more than 16 percent of GDP. In the developing countries the expansion of foreign direct investment was less pronounced, from about 7 percent to 17 percent of GDP, while foreign equity investment—which was close to zero in 1970—increased to about 3 percent of GDP in 1998. See also IMF (2001, chap. 4) for a discussion of the rise in capital mobility and its effects on growth.

11. Barro, Mankiw, and Sala-i-Martin (1995) proposed an alternative explanation. In order to attract foreign capital, a country needs to provide collateral, and only physical capital can serve this purpose. As a result, poor countries that have little physical capital cannot attract much foreign investment. I do not find this explanation convincing.

12. For a sample of twenty-two OECD countries the equation performs poorly; it explains only 1 percent of the variation. One important dif-

ference between the two samples is that within the group of OECD countries there is little variation in rates of population growth as compared to the larger sample.

### 3. PRODUCTIVITY

1. As is well known, there are forms of factor-augmenting changes in technology that are equivalent to Hicks-neutral technological change. This is the case, for example, when there are constant returns to scale in production and the productivity of all inputs is augmented at the same rate. Or when the production function is Cobb-Douglas, because then every input-augmenting change in technology has a Hicks-neutral equivalent rate of technological change.

2. Abramovitz (1956) was earlier, but Solow developed the analytical apparatus that turned growth accounting into a powerful empirical instrument.

3. More accurately, the contribution of the input equals the elasticity of the output level with respect to the input multiplied by the rate of growth of the input. In a competitive economy with constant returns to scale in production, however, the elasticity of output with respect to an input equals the input's share in GDP. For this reason input shares, which can be calculated from national income accounts, are used instead of the elasticities.

4. Productivity growth was uneven during 1960–1995. It was much faster during 1960–1972 than during 1973–1995, and TFP contributed a larger fraction to output growth in the earlier period.

5. For Hong Kong the period is 1966–1991.

6. During these years Korean output grew at 10.3 percent per annum; Hong Kong's output grew at 7.3 percent. These were the fastest and the slowest growth rates of output in the group.

7. Note that the calculation of TFP growth, as the difference between the rate of growth of output and the weighted average of the rate of growth of inputs, aggregates the contributions of Hicks-neutral technical change, labor-augmenting technical change, and capital-

augmenting technical change. It therefore represents growth in aggregate efficiency.

8. Blomström, Lipsey and Zejan (1996) provided evidence that in a large sample of countries, growth of income per capita preceded capital accumulation, but they found no evidence that capital accumulation preceded growth. These findings are consistent with the view that productivity growth drives investment.

9. Interestingly, differences in productivity growth are not limited to mixed samples of rich and poor countries. Jorgenson and Yip (2001) showed that even within the group of the seven largest economies, the G7, there were substantial differences in the levels of TFP in the early sixties, and that these differences have declined over time because of faster productivity growth in the lower-productivity countries within the group.

10. A high correlation between TFP growth and growth of the capital-labor ratio was reported by Baumol, Blackman, and Wolff (1989) for seven OECD countries over the period 1880–1979.

11. Islam (1995) used a panel approach and he did not account for education differences across countries. He estimated the TFP levels with fixed country effects. When he did not use fixed effects, his estimated capital share was similar to the capital share estimated by Mankiw, Romer, and Weil when they too did not control for education. Namely, the estimated capital share was unreasonably high. But this share dropped to reasonable levels when he introduced fixed effects. So this approach too points to the importance of allowing for productivity differences across countries.

12. Islam estimated the 1960 productivity levels under the assumption that the rate of productivity growth is the same in all countries. If the latter assumption is correct, then the productivity ratios are the same in every year and therefore the 1960 ratios also equal the average ratios. Since the assumption of a common rate of productivity growth is not consistent with the evidence, it is better to interpret his estimates as the average productivity levels over the 1960–1985 period.

13. Hall and Jones (1999) provided estimates for 1988. They adjusted la-

bor input for quality by giving higher weight to workers with more years of schooling. Relying on estimates from wage regressions reported in Psacharopoulos (1994), they used a 13.4 percent return on a year of schooling for workers with zero to four years of schooling, 10.1 percent for workers with four to eight years of schooling, and 6.8 percent for workers with more than eight years of schooling. Hall and Jones also reported large differences in the level of output per worker in their sample of 127 countries. For example, the five richest countries had in 1988 a geometric mean of output per worker that was almost thirty-two times higher than the geometric mean of output per worker in the five poorest countries.

14. Growth accounting was used to calculate these rates of TFP growth, without adjusting for labor and capital qualities. They are an updated version of the rates of TFP growth from Coe and Helpman (1995).

15. Caselli, Esquivel, and Lefort (1996) found a similar relationship between TFP and income per capita.

16. This is similar to the index of human capital constructed by Hall and Jones (1999), although the two studies do not use identical rates of return to education. There is a controversy concerning how to best measure the contribution of human capital to the growth of income. See Krueger and Lindhal (2001) and Cohen and Soto (2001) for a discussion.

17. Easterly and Levine (2001) reported that TFP growth explains about 60 percent of the variation in the growth rate of income per capita in their sample. The exact number depends on the sample period and the countries sampled.

## 4. INNOVATION

1. Using estimates from Maddison (1982), Romer (1986) reported that the average annual rate of growth was −0.07 percent in the Netherlands between 1700 and 1785, 0.5 percent in the UK between 1785 and 1820, 1.4 percent in the UK between 1820 and 1890, and 2.3 per-

cent in the United States between 1890 and 1979. The data used to construct Figure 1.5 were not available at the time.

2. The starting point is important for this argument, because the U.S. growth rate of GDP per capita has not been rising since the middle of the nineteenth century. As is evident from Figure 1.5, however, the United States is an exception; the average rate of growth of the world economy has been rising since the middle of the nineteenth century.

3. Solow's model can also give rise to a long-run growth rate that exceeds the rate of technological change. This happens when the marginal productivity of capital does not decline to zero as the capital stock grows without bound. This point was recognized by Solow in his 1956 article, and it was used by various authors to construct models in which the growth rate stays above the rate of productivity growth. In this case, however, the growth rate has to decline over time. For an early example, see Jones and Manuelli (1990).

4. Goldin and Katz (2001) found that from 1915 to 1999 the wage-weighted index of years of schooling increased at the rate of 0.53 percent per annum. Taking a labor share (the share of Labor income in GDP) of 0.7, they used growth accounting to attribute to education the rate $0.7 \times 0.53 = 0.37$ percent of output growth. For a similar span of time, Gordon (2000) estimated a rate of growth of output per unit labor of 1.62 percent. Therefore education contributed the fraction 0.37/1.62, which equals 23 percent, to the growth of output per worker. Using the same sources and the same type of calculation, I find that during the first half of the twentieth century the contribution of education is a little lower, about 21 percent. The difference stems mostly from the faster growth of output during the earlier period.

5. Hanushek and Kimko (2000) found that, controlling for years of schooling, cross-country variation in productivity depends on the quality of schooling. They used scores in standardized tests as proxies for school quality.

6. Mokyr (2002) provides a historical account of the role of knowledge in the development of the West. His account is replete with examples

of external effects, such as the publication of the first encyclopedia. These externalities have been very important, even if we do not have a quantitative assessment of their size.

7. A summary of the evidence is provided in Mohnen (1992).

8. See Terleckyj (1980), Scherer (1982), Griliches (1992), and Mohnen (1992). Both Terleckyj and Scherer found social rates of return to R&D in excess of 100 percent and private rates of return of 25 percent and 29 percent, respectively. Their estimates show that the external effects are larger than the internal effects by a factor of three, implying that the external effects are very large indeed.

9. In an open economy, the link between saving and investment is weakened by the presence of international capital flows. Yet investment equals saving in the aggregate, for the world economy. Therefore the link between saving and growth can be weaker in individual countries than in the world economy.

10. Since the mere registration of a patent discloses valuable information, companies do not always patent inventions in order to avoid the revelation of nonpatentable features of their technologies.

11. The quality-ladder models formalize Schumpeter's (1942) notion of "creative destruction." Segerstrom, Anant, and Dinopoulos (1990) provided an early version of a model of this type.

12. See Grossman and Helpman (1991b, chap. 4) for a discussion of these points. Despite this similarity, each one of the models emphasizes an important distinct mechanism of growth, which explains why they have been widely used. Aghion and Howitt (forthcoming) review several applications of the model of quality ladders.

13. Jones (2002) used a second-generation model of endogenous growth, which contains modifications that were triggered by the criticism described in the next section.

14. Note, however, that Kremer (1993) found that over a very long time span the growth rate was positively correlated with population size.

15. The initial response of economists was to attribute the productivity slowdown to the oil crisis. In retrospect it is clear that, even if the oil crisis triggered the slowdown, it could not have been responsible for

its prolonged duration. I will provide a technological explanation in the next section. Much controversy still surrounds the causes of this productivity slowdown. Griliches (2000, chap. 5) reviewed some pertinent aspects of the debate.

16. Grossman and Helpman (1991b, chap. 5) discuss the relevant scale variable in some detail. In particular, they argue that whenever R&D is skill intensive, low elasticities of substitution between skilled and unskilled workers in the major activities may lead to situations in which countries with larger amounts of unskilled labor grow more slowly. So this is a case in which size does not feed faster growth. But no matter what these elasticities are, countries with more skilled workers should grow more quickly. The implication is that the theoretical models do not predict a positive correlation between country size (as measured by GDP) and the rate of productivity growth, but they do predict a positive correlation between measures of size that are important for R&D and the rate of productivity growth. This argument does not resolve, however, the point made by Jones concerning the correlation between the number of scientists and engineers employed in R&D and the rate of productivity growth. Grossman and Helpman (1991b, app. A3.1) also discuss the ways in which the scale effect depends on features of the public knowledge accumulation function. In particular, they derive conditions under which the rate of productivity growth approaches a positive value in the long run, and conditions under which it approaches zero.

17. Young allowed forward spillovers from quality-improving R&D but not from R&D designed to invent new products. This distinction is important for his results. When forward spillovers in the invention of new products are introduced into his model, the effects of scale on the long-run rate of productivity growth are restored.

18. Howitt (2000) also used a hybrid of Solow and first-generation endogenous growth models to derive empirical equations that are similar to the equations that Mankiw, Romer, and Weil (1992) derived from Solow's model. In Howitt's model, R&D drives productivity growth, but technological diffusion spreads the R&D benefits across

all countries and thereby ties their long-run rates of growth. R&D-performing countries converge to parallel growth trajectories, on which relative incomes per capital are constant. Countries that do not invest in R&D stagnate. Unlike the first-generation models, however, this one predicts that a country with a higher saving rate will have a higher income per capita in the long run, but that its long-run growth rate will not deviate from the growth rate of the other R&D-performing countries. On the other hand, the common long-run growth rate of the R&D-performing countries is higher the higher their saving rates. Cross-country variations in R&D subsidies have similar implications. It is important to note, however, that these implications result in large measure from the assumption that R&D spillovers are international in scope, as will be explained in the next chapter.

19. Alesina, Spolaore, and Wacziarg (2003) estimate significant scale effects when accounting for the interaction between foreign trade and the size of countries.

20. See von Tunzelmann (1978) on the steam engine, Du Boff (1967) on electricity, and David (1991) on the similarity between electricity and the computer. The adjustment to the steam engine lasted more than a century; the adjustment to electricity lasted more than four decades. It is not yet clear how long the adjustment to the computer will last.

21. See Lipsey, Bekar, and Carlaw (1998) for a discussion of GPTs in a historical perspective, and Helpman (1998) for a collection of essays that examine various aspects of this type of technology.

22. This figure describes the quarterly ratios of corporate equities, issued at market value, to GDP. The value of equities is from the Flow of Fund Accounts, Table L213, Federal Reserve Board of Governors; the GDP data are from the Bureau of Economic Analysis. I am grateful to Bart Hobijn from the Federal Reserve Board of Governors for supplying these data, which were also used by Greenwood and Jovanovic.

23. In the last quarter of 1999 and the first quarter of 2000 market capitalization was twice the GDP level, and it fell after that. Many con-

sider the second half of the nineties to be a period in which there was a bubble in asset markets. This bubble does not detract, however, from the significance of the cyclical pattern portrayed in the figure.

## 5. INTERDEPENDENCE

1. I thank Alan Taylor for providing the data for Figure 5.1.

2. A country's terms of trade are defined as the ratio of a price index of its exportables to a price index of its importables.

3. Schott (2003) showed that countries were indeed located in different regions of diversification.

4. Bhagwati (1958) noted that a growing country can suffer a severe enough deterioration in its terms of trade so as to lose from its own growth. The required condition for this unfortunate outcome is a low enough elasticity of demand for the country's exports. Empirical estimates of import demand elasticities show, however, that this condition is not satisfied in practice.

5. See Bardhan (1970).

6. Irwin and Klenow (1994) found, for example, that in the semiconductor industry learning spilled over to firms in foreign countries as much as it did across firms in the home country.

7. This argument applies to the growth rates of real GDP. Because of shifts in the terms of trade, however, the rate of growth of real GDP is not the same as the rate of growth of real consumption, because real GDP is computed with a GDP deflator while real consumption is computed with a consumer price index (CPI), which contains prices of imported products that are absent from the GDP deflator.

8. Lucas (1988) reached a similar conclusion in his analysis of a world with two goods and many countries. He showed that trade locks in the initial patterns of specialization when the elasticity of substitution between the products exceeds one. In this case growth rates of output per capita do not converge. Countries that specialize in the product that has the higher growth potential grow faster; those that specialize in the other product grow more slowly. Matsuyama (1992)

also developed a two-sector model—which he interpreted to represent agriculture and manufacturing—in which there is learning-by-doing in one sector only, manufacturing. In this model trade speeds up growth when it raises the relative price of manufactures and it slows down growth when it reduces this relative price.

9. Grossman and Helpman (1995) review the literature on learning-by-doing and international interdependence, as well as the literature on innovation and international interdependence. They discuss a variety of mechanisms that I have ignored.

10. Learning-by-doing can be purposeful as well. When companies recognize that experience affects their productivity, they have an incentive to expand their activities beyond short-run profitability considerations. In these circumstances companies invest in learning-by-doing. This investment is not different from other types of investment so long as the return to learning-by-doing is company specific. For this reason the literature on learning-by-doing and my discussion in the text focus on learning that has external effects.

11. Aghion, Harris, Howitt, and Vickers (2001) developed a model in which more competition reduces profits and thereby the incentive to innovate, but at the same time more competition encourages firms to distance themselves from the nearest rivals and thereby raises the incentive to innovate. In principle either one of these forces can dominate. In these authors' model, however, the latter typically has the stronger impact, producing a positive link between the degree of competitive pressure and the rate of innovation and growth.

12. When opening to trade reduces the relative price of the human-capital-intensive product, human capital becomes cheaper and R&D costs fall. As a result, investment in R&D becomes more profitable, R&D expands, and TFP growth accelerates. If trade raises the relative price of the human-capital-intensive product, R&D costs rise, R&D investment declines, and TFP growth slows down.

13. Trade expands the available brands of both inputs and final goods. The broadening of the availability of either inputs or final goods pro-

duces gains from trade. See Helpman and Krugman (1985, chaps. 9 and 11) for a discussion of these points.

14. See also Howitt (2000) for an integration of such convergence forces into an otherwise neoclassical multicountry model of economic growth.

15. This factor price equalization result is reminiscent of the static factor price equalization theorem, which is a cornerstone of the Heckscher-Ohlin trade theory. Note, however, that in the dynamic version discussed in the text, the result applies only to the long-run equilibrium. In fact, when the countries open to trade, factor prices need not fully converge in the short run, even when the countries have similar factor endowments. The reason is that the number of products that they know how to produce need not be aligned with their differences in factor availability. But as long as the R&D stocks of knowledge are shared worldwide, R&D investment in product development leads to the eventual alignment of the numbers of products with the available inputs, and to factor price equalization. See Grossman and Helpman (1991b, chap. 7).

16. When the two countries differ greatly in size and the smaller country has an initial advantage in the R&D stock of knowledge, it is possible for the larger country to take over the smaller country as the leader in the R&D stock of knowledge. Under these circumstances the initial conditions do not fully determine the equilibrium trajectory.

17. See Rosenberg and Birdzell (1986, chaps. 2 and 3).

18. Galor and Mountford (2003) provide an analysis in which the specialization patterns interact with demographics. This interaction produces growth divergence together with a demographic transition in Europe and lagging growth in East Asia.

19. Edwards (1993) reviewed the early literature.

20. The same result obtains when the ratio of imports to GDP is used as the measure of openness, or when imports plus exports relative to GDP are used as the measure of openness.

21. Among the geographic characteristics they included the land area,

whether a country is landlocked, and whether the trading partners have a common border.

22. Frankel and Romer (1999) used data from 1985. Irwin and Terviö (2002) expanded their analysis to various other years in the twentieth century and found similar results. Irwin and Terviö also noted that the results are not robust to the inclusion of the distance from the equator as an additional geographic characteristic.

23. Frankel and Romer also examined the effects of openness on the rate of growth of income per capita in the working paper that preceded the published version of their paper (see Frankel and Romer 1996). They found there that openness has a strong effect on the growth rate. Moreover, the effect of trade on the growth *rate* was estimated with considerably more precision than the effect of trade on the *level* of per capita income.

24. Larger countries tend to be less exposed to foreign trade. For this reason it is important to carefully isolate the effect of trade from the effect of size.

25. Mali's population was estimated to exceed 11 million in 2002. Seychelles is an archipelago in the western part of the Indian Ocean. Its population was estimated to be around 80,000 in 2002. See the CIA, World Factbook 2002, at *www.cia.gov/cia/publications/factbook/geos/se.html.*

26. O'Rourke's sample consists of developed European and non-European countries: Australia, Canada, Denmark, France, Germany, Italy, Norway, Sweden, the United Kingdom, and the United States.

27. The countries are: Argentina, Australia, Austria, Brazil, Burma, Canada, Ceylon, Chile, China, Colombia, Cuba, Denmark, Egypt, France, Germany, Greece, India, Indonesia, Italy, Japan, Mexico, New Zealand, Norway, Peru, the Philippines, Portugal, Russia, Spain, Sweden, Thailand, Turkey, United Kingdom, United States, Uruguay, Yugoslavia (Serbia). I thank Michael Clemens and Jeffrey Williamson for the data for this figure.

28. Little progress was achieved in the Dillon Round of trade negotiations in 1960–1961, but tariffs were reduced by 35 percent in the

Kennedy Round (1962-1967), by an additional 33 percent in the To-kyo Round (1973-1979), and they were further reduced to just a few percent on trade in manufactures in the Uruguay Round (1986-1994).

29. See, for example, Dollar (1992), Ben-David (1993), and Sachs and Warner (1995).

30. See Leamer (1988).

31. Apart from the accumulation variables, all other variables affect growth through TFP. Although some of Wacziarg's variables closely approximate the desired channel of influence, such as the share of government consumption in GDP as a measure of the size of government, others do not. Particularly unsatisfactory is the use of manufactured exports in total merchandise exports as a proxy for technology transmission.

32. The constructed R&D capital stocks do not appear to be particularly sensitive to the rate of depreciation.

33. This rate of return in the large industrial countries is comparable to the rate of return estimated by Scherer (1982).

34. Using data from OECD countries, Eaton and Kortum (1996, 1999) estimated a quality-ladder-type growth model in which cross-border patenting diffuses ideas, and they found significant productivity spillovers across countries. For example, in Eaton and Kortum (1996)—where they studied nineteen OECD countries—they found that all countries but one, the United States, obtained more than 50 percent of their productivity growth from ideas that originated abroad. And excluding the United States, Japan, Germany, France, and the UK—the leaders in R&D—the remaining countries obtained more than 90 percent of their productivity growth from ideas that originated abroad. Finally, Eaton and Kortum found that distance between countries inhibited the flow of ideas while trade relationships enhanced them.

35. It is important to note that the "absorptive capacity" of foreign technologies differs across countries, and that investment in R&D designed to improve the use of foreign technologies can be as pro-

ductive in lagging countries as inventive activities are in leading countries. Caselli and Coleman (2001) showed, for example, that imports per worker of computer equipment varied greatly across countries between 1970 and 1990. Since there were few suppliers of such equipment, one can interpret imports of this equipment as indicators of technology imports. Caselli and Coleman found that countries with better-educated workers had higher imports. That is, education contributed to absorptive capacity. Griffith, Redding, and Reenen (2003) provided additional evidence on this issue. Examining growth of TFP, they found that countries that lagged behind the technology frontier tended to catch up with the leading countries, and that the rate at which they caught up was higher the more they invested in R&D. R&D helped laggards to faster catch up with the technology frontier.

36. See Engelbrecht (1997), Keller (1998), and Lichtenberg and van Pottelsberghe de la Potterie (1998).

37. Hejazi and Safarian (1999) incorporated foreign direct investment into the Coe-Helpman framework and found that international spillovers from FDI to TFP are at least as large as the spillovers from trade to TFP. Bernstein and Mohnen (1998) found large spillovers between the United States and Japan in high-technology sectors. They estimated that international spillovers made the social rate of return to investment in R&D four times larger than the private rate of return.

   Not all studies find a positive effect of FDI on productivity, however. For a balanced survey of the literature, see Fan (2002).

38. Since Keller accounted only for the composition of trade and FDI, but not for their levels, these estimates may be biased.

## 6. INEQUALITY

1. Kuznets used the income shares of the richest 20 percent of the population and the poorest 60 percent of the population to measure income inequality. Income inequality is greater the larger the share of

the richest fraction of the population and the smaller the share of the poorest fraction of the population.

2. See Paukert (1973) for a study of fifty-six countries.

3. Lindert and Williamson (1985) examined historical data for a small sample of European countries and the United States. They found no evidence of a Kuznets Curve.

4. See Deininger and Squire (1998) and Lundberg and Squire (2003).

5. The upper bounds differ, however. While the Gini coefficient has an upper bound of one, the upper bound of the Theil index is larger the larger the population.

6. See Bourguignon (1979) for a theoretical analysis of decomposable properties of inequality measures and Conçeicão and Ferreira (2000) for a discussion of the decomposability properties of the Theil index, with applications to income distribution around the world.

7. Dynan, Skinner, and Zeldes (forthcoming) found that in the United States the marginal propensity to save rises with individual lifetime income. But Schmidt-Hebbel and Serven (2000) found no statistically significant link between income inequality and aggregate saving in a cross section of countries.

8. This statement needs to be qualified for small economies with unrestricted international capital flows. When an economy is large or there is friction in the flow of international capital, higher domestic savings raise domestic investment.

9. Galor and Zeira (1993) provided the first analysis of a link between inequality and growth in the presence of credit constraints. They assumed nondivisible investment projects. Later studies showed that this mechanism also works when investment projects are divisible; see Piketty (1997) and Galor and Moav (forthcoming).

10. The preferences of the median voter are most easily defined over a policy that has one dimension only, such as the size of the education budget or the level of a tariff. The median voter is identified as the person whose most preferred choice is such that half of the remaining voters prefer a higher value and the other half prefer a lower value. When every voter has a well-defined best choice and the prefer-

ences of everyone have a single peak, then the policy most preferred by the median voter wins a majority over every other policy in a bilateral contest. Moreover, when two candidates compete for votes, then under these circumstances both are inclined to offer the policy that is most preferred by the median voter. These insights have been used to justify the most preferred policy of the median voter as the policy outcome in a democratic society. Many authors have shown, however, that important deviations from this prediction emerge when the decision-making process is more realistically structured. See Grossman and Helpman (2001, part I) for an overview of these issues.

11. Note that distortions do not necessarily reduce the rate of growth; they may, for example, only reduce the level of real income. For this reason the distortions need to be of a particular kind in order to slow growth.

12. Persson and Tabellini (1992) also reported a negative effect of the Gini coefficient of land distribution on growth.

13. They used regional dummies for Latin America, Africa, and Asia.

14. Perotti (1996) also found a weak negative effect of income inequality on growth. But Forbes (2000) found a positive effect in the short and medium term, when estimating the relationship with panel data and fixed country effects.

15. The correlation between Deininger and Squire's Gini coefficients of income inequality and land ownership inequality was 0.39 for the sample of countries for which both measures were available. These two measures of inequality thus seem to be only moderately correlated.

16. This measure is equal to the broad monetary aggregate M2 relative to GDP. M2 consists of the money supply, M1, plus other less liquid deposits in the banking system (savings and small time deposits, overnight repos at commercial banks, and noninstitutional money market accounts). M1 consists of coin, currency held by the public, traveler's checks, checking account balances, NOW accounts, automatic transfer service accounts, and balances in credit unions.

17. Banerjee and Duflo (2003) provide important qualifications to this conclusion. They argue convincingly that the linear relationships between inequality and growth used in earlier studies is misspecified, and that the data seem to suggest that *changes* in inequality hurt growth.

18. See, for example, Acemoglu (2002a). The decline of the real wages of unskilled workers is large when the official CPI is used as the deflator. But a 1 percent adjustment for quality, as proposed by the Boskin Commission, implies roughly constant real wages for the low-skill workers.

19. The relative supply of skills is defined in this figure as weeks worked by college equivalents relative to weeks worked by noncollege equivalents, while the skill premium is the log of college wages relative to noncollege wages. I thank Daron Acemoglu for providing the data for this figure.

20. See the early study by Katz and Murphy (1992) and the review of the literature by Katz and Autor (1999), as well as Acemoglu (2002a, 2003).

21. Additional explanations that were offered in the literature include: a deceleration in the growth of the relative supply of college graduates, by Katz and Murphy (1992); changes in labor market institutions that weakened the labor unions, by DiNardo, Fortin, and Lemieux (1996); and the acceleration of technological change, which temporarily raises the demand for skilled workers, by Galor and Tsiddon (1997) and Caselli (1999). See Aghion, Caroli, and García-Peñalosa (1999) for a review of some of these issues.

22. As is well known from trade theory, in a constant-returns-to-scale two-sector, two-factor economy, an increase in the relative price of a good raises the real reward of the input that is used intensively in the production of this good and reduces the real reward of the input that is used intensively in the production of the other good. This is known as the Stolper-Samuelson theorem; see Stolper and Samuelson (1941).

23. See Wood (1994) and Leamer (1998).

24. See Katz and Murphy (1992), Krugman (1995) and Katz and Autor (1999). In a closed economic system skill-biased technological change raises the effective supply of skilled labor. The larger number of effective units of skilled labor leads in turn to a decline in the remuneration of every effective unit. But the fall in this remuneration is proportionately smaller than the rise in quantity. Therefore the real wage of every skilled worker—who is now endowed with more effective units—rises. Under these circumstances the real wage of unskilled workers does not decline, however, unless a larger supply of skill reduces their marginal productivity. The three-factor two-technology model of Beaudry and Green (2003) does in fact predict a negative impact of human capital on the wages of unskilled workers. In their model the inputs are unskilled labor, human capital, and physical capital. The two technologies are an old technology and a new one. Real wages fall for unskilled workers when the new technology is substantially more skill intensive than the old technology. They fall in particular when the new technology uses human capital and physical capital while the old technology uses unskilled labor and physical capital. Under these circumstances an increase in human capital leads to a reallocation of physical capital from the old to the new technology. As a result, unskilled workers have less capital to work with in activities that employ the old technology, leading to a decline in their wage. Caselli (1999) provided a similar argument.

25. An assessment of the size of the decline in the relative price of products that were unskilled-labor intensive during the period under consideration is of major importance to the trade argument. Was it small or large? Although some controversy surrounds this issue, most of the evidence suggests that the relative price movement was only modest in comparison with what is needed to explain the shift in relative wages. See Lawrence and Slaughter (1993) for evidence of small price changes and Leamer (1998) for a contrary view. A good summary of this evidence is provided in Slaughter (2000).

26. These results obtain in a standard Heckscher-Ohlin model of international trade.

27. See, for example, Berman, Bound, and Griliches (1994) and Autor, Katz, and Krueger (1998).

28. I have excluded Norway, Japan, and Germany from the figure, because for each of these countries data are missing for one of the decades. For Norway no share is available for the 1980s, but the share in the 1970s was 81 percent. For Japan no share is available for the 1970s, but the share in the 1980s was over 100 percent. For Germany no share is available for the 1980s, but the share in the 1970s was 93 percent. I also excluded Luxembourg, for which the share in the 1980s exceeded 100 percent.

29. This view gains additional support from Desjonqueres, Machin, and Van Reenen (1999) and Berman and Machin (2000), who showed that skill upgrading within industries was also pervasive in developing countries, though not in the poorest of them. Desjonqueres, Machin, and Van Reenen reported, for example, that in Brazil, Chile, Colombia, Ecuador, and Pakistan the fraction of the rise in the share of skilled workers that is attributable to within-industry changes in employment exceeded 80 percent, and only in India was it substantially lower, 38.4 percent. They also showed that in the industrial countries the changes in the within-industry employment shares of skilled workers were not correlated with rising imports from less-developed countries, which undermines the trade argument.

30. The factor content of trade consists of the quantities of inputs that are embodied in the net trade flows. The use of these quantities by Borjas, Freeman, and Katz (1997) as implicit changes in factor endowments for the calculation of implied changes in wages is justified under Krugman's (2000) assumptions but not under Leamer's (2000). I side with Krugman on this issue. Nevertheless, I believe that these calculations are only rough approximations, not so much due to their theoretical deficiency, but rather due to the empirical difficulty of calculating suitable measures of factor use per unit output. To overcome this obstacle, Borjas, Freeman, and Katz (1997) examined the sensitivity of their results to alternative assumptions about these factor intensity measures.

31. This elasticity of substitution was estimated by Katz and Murphy (1992). Although a range of estimates exists for this elasticity, 1.4 is within the acceptable range.

32. See also Feenstra and Hanson (1996, 1999) for the evolution of their theoretical arguments and empirical estimates.

33. I should add that the argument that this segmentation of the production process was enabled by technological developments is no less compelling than the argument that it was enabled by falling trade barriers. Both were important. Therefore I see the Feenstra-Hanson position as being driven not by pure trade considerations, but rather by a combination of trade and technology.

34. The shifting of production of low-skill–intensive activities to the South can take place via foreign direct investment or arm's-length trade. Both types of foreign sourcing grew during the 1980s and 1990s. Although Feenstra and Hanson emphasized the FDI channel in their earlier studies, in Feenstra and Hanson (2003) they placed significant weight on the trade channel. See also Trefler and Zhu (2001) for an interesting analysis of the trade channel.

35. Note that different studies have used different measures of the relative wage of skilled workers. The most suitable measure is the average wage of workers with an education level above some threshold relative to the average wage of workers with lower education. But the data needed for this type of analysis have not always been available. Therefore researchers have often used instead the average wage of nonproduction workers relative to the average wage of production workers as a measure of the relative wage of skilled workers. This measure presumes that nonproduction workers are better educated than production workers.

36. Griliches (1969) was the first to propose this distinction, and many followed in his footsteps.

37. Beaudry and Green (2003) made a similar point in their comparison of the United States and Germany.

38. See Greenwood, Hercowitz, and Krusell (1997).

39. Jorgenson (n.d.) reassessed the effects of IT equipment on the growth

of the G7 countries. He found that not only was investment in IT equipment responsible for the acceleration of U.S. growth between 1995 and 2000, but that it also was responsible for an acceleration of growth of the other G7 countries (except Italy) when suitably revised data are used. See also Jorgenson (2001) for a discussion of the U.S. experience with IT equipment and the methodology to estimate its effects.

40. See Acemoglu (2002b) for a detailed analysis.

41. These are standard measures of poverty that have been developed by the World Bank.

42. The exact figures of these poverty indexes are sensitive to data sets and estimation methodologies. They are particularly sensitive to the ways in which income distribution is represented—that is, whether one uses a continuous distribution or a rough measure such as deciles. In the latter case it is typically assumed, as did Bourguignon and Morrisson (2002), that all individuals in the same decile have the same income level. The time trend of these measures does not appear to be sensitive to the estimation method, however. See Sala-i-Martin (2002) for a discussion of these points. He also provided a set of estimates from 1970 to 1998 that rely on the entire distribution of income. His poverty measures are much smaller than Bourguignon and Morrisson's. For example, while Bourguignon and Morrisson estimated that in 1992, 51.3 percent of the world's population lived on less than $2 a day and 23.7 percent lived on less than $1 a day, Sala-i-Martin (2002) estimated that in 1992, 23.9 percent of the world's population lived on less than $2 a day and only 8 percent lived on less than $1 a day.

43. Growth in Latin America also contributed to poverty reduction during certain periods of time, while negative growth in Africa contributed to rising poverty. The poverty trends differed greatly across regions; see Sala-i-Martin (2002).

44. This figure is constructed from 418 observations of 137 countries. The number of observations is not the same for all countries, however. For some countries there is only one observation, for others a

larger number. The median number of observations per country is 3. I am grateful to Aart Kraay for providing the data for this figure.

45. I have discussed some of these variables, such as measures of trade openness, including tariffs and trade volumes, in previous chapters.

46. See also Deininger and Squire (1996) and Ravallion and Chen (1997).

## 7. INSTITUTIONS AND POLITICS

1. See Caselli and Coleman (2003) for estimates of the world technology frontier and Acemoglu, Aghion, and Zilibotti (2002, 2003) for an analysis of forces that shape the evolution of the frontier and individual country TFP levels.

2. Dixit (forthcoming) provided an illuminating analysis of the roles of private institutions in cultivating economic activity.

3. Khan and Sokoloff (2001) describe how market size affected the evolution of the U.S. patent system and how this system contributed to the rapid growth of inventions in the nineteenth century.

4. Arrow (1974, p. 33) took a somewhat different view of organizations: "Organizations are a means of achieving the benefits of collective action in situations in which the price system fails . . . the term, 'organizations,' should be interpreted quite broadly. Formal organizations, firms, labor unions, university, or government, are not the only kind. Ethical codes and the market system itself are to be interpreted as organizations; the market system, indeed, has elaborate methods for communication and joint decision-making." Arrow singled out the roles of uncertainty and information in the formation of organizations, as did North (1981, 1990), who followed Arrow in the inclusion of formal and informal entities in their definition.

5. See Greif (n.d., chap. 5).

6. See also Greif (n.d., chap. 3).

7. Most of the historical records for this study came from the Cairo *geniza*, which is a collection of original documents that includes contracts, accounts, and correspondence among traders.

8. Greif (1993) constructed a repeated game which has this as an equilibrium outcome. That is, when everyone plays the equilibrium strategy, it is a best response to inform the community about a dishonest agent and not to deal with a dishonest agent.

9. Naturally, in every community local residents could use the local court to enforce the commitments of other local residents.

10. They also found that higher procedural formalism leads to lower honesty, consistency, and fairness of the system.

11. Using the Djankov, La Porta, Lopez-de-Silanes and Shleifer measures of entry barriers, Acemoglu, Aghion, and Zilibotti (2003) found that for countries with low entry barriers there is a weak negative relationship between the growth rate and the country's distance to the technology frontier, while for countries with high entry barriers there is a strong negative relationship. This evidence suggests that entry regulation reduces the rate of catch-up to the technology frontier, and that the regulations are more harmful the closer a country is to the frontier.

12. The findings on the regulation of labor markets are reported in Botero et al. (2003).

13. A similar role is sometimes attributed to culture; see Landes (1998). Although cultural factors, embedded in social norms, may well be important for growth, we do not have good quantitative assessments of their influence.

14. The British empire had a federal structure, which provided a credible commitment mechanism for the respect of property rights, while the Spanish empire relied on the Church, the army, and the nobility to maintain political stability. As a result, "Spanish mercantilism appears designed to maximize the crown's extraction from the new world, at considerable cost to economic development of the empire. In contrast, the British empire's federal structure seems close to a system designed to maximize economic development within the empire" (North, Summerhill, and Weingast 2000, 34–35).

15. They calculated the average value of this index during 1985–1995 for every country in the sample and correlated this average with the mor-

tality rate. Their data cover sixty-four countries in different parts of the world (the Americas, Asia, Africa, and Australasia) that were colonized by the Europeans.

16. They also reported the relationship between settler mortality rates and other measures of institutional quality, such as constraints on the executive.

17. The share of the population living in a temperate zone also has a positive impact on infant mortality and life expectancy, after the effect of income per capita is controlled for.

18. Their other instruments were the fraction of the population speaking English as the mother tongue, the fraction of the population speaking one of the five primary European languages as the mother tongue, and the predicted trade share from Frankel and Romer (1999) (see Chapter 5 for a discussion of the last variable).

19. Unlike later periods, direct measures of income per capita do not exist circa the discovery of the New World.

20. I thank Daron Acemoglu and Simon Johnson for providing the data for this figure.

21. This is consistent with the arguments in Engerman and Sokoloff (1997) and Sokoloff and Engerman (2000).

22. Again in line with the arguments in Engerman and Sokoloff (1997) and Sokoloff and Engerman (2000).

23. This is also in line with the results in Acemoglu, Aghion, and Zilibotti (2003).

24. Important early cross-country studies of the effects of institutions on growth were Knack and Keefer (1995) and Mauro (1995); both showed positive effects of good institutions on growth. These studies introduced data that were used extensively by later authors.

25. Easterly and Levine (2003) also argued that policies have no direct effect on development when institutions are controlled for. This point is disputed by Rodrik, Subramanian, and Trebbi (2002), however, on econometric grounds.

26. In contrast, Barro (1997, chap. 2) argued that in countries with few political rights the growth rate rises with the index of political rights

while in countries with many political rights the growth rate declines with the index of political rights. Namely, there is an inverted U-shaped relationship between the growth rate and political rights. Importantly, this relationship emerges after controlling for initial income per capita, education, life expectancy, an index of the rule of law, and other determinants of economic growth. The inverted U-shaped relationship is not particularly strong, however.

27. See Rodrik (1999).

28. See Przeworski et al. (2000, fig. 2.1).

29. See ibid., table 2.10.

30. See ibid., chap. 3, and Barro (1997, chap. 2). After controlling for initial income per capita, education, and other variables, Barro found an inverted U-shaped relationship between the investment rate and the index of political rights.

31. Their analysis admits only two types of regimes, so the transition is either from democracy to nondemocracy or vice versa.

32. It is interesting to note, however, that regime types had strong effects on economic development in historical perspective. De Long and Shleifer (1993) studied the relationship between regime types and the growth of cities from the Middle Ages to the nineteenth century. They found that cities grew much more slowly under absolutist regimes, in which all the power was concentrated in the hands of the prince, than under other regimes in which power was more diffused, such as city-states that were dominated by merchants.

33. Acemoglu and Robinson (2003) provide numerous historical examples in support of various parts of their theory. They also discuss the collapse of democratic regimes, the role of the middle class, reasons for waves of democratization, and the role of globalization in regime switches.

34. We encountered the Stolper-Samuelson theorem in Chapter 5. In its simplest form it states that, in a two-sector two-factor economy with labor and capital, an increase in the relative price of capital-intensive goods will raise the real income of capital and reduce the real income of labor. And similarly, an increase in the relative price of labor-inten-

sive goods will raise the real income of labor and reduce the real income of capital. More sophisticated versions admit more inputs and outputs.

35. Rogowski (1989) also applied this type of analysis to the interwar era, the post–World War II era, and historical episodes in ancient Greece, the Roman Empire, and sixteenth-century Europe.

36. Grossman and Helpman (1996) showed in turn how the weight attached to welfare relative to contributions depends on characteristics of the polity.

37. These are typically structural estimates that follow the original outline in Goldberg and Maggi (1999). See Gawande and Krishna (2003) for a review of this literature.

38. Special interests have many dimensions, as a result of which different groups choose to interact with the political system in different ways. The impact of these activities on economic growth is not well understood. For example, studies of the link between social fragmentation and growth find that more fragmented societies grow more slowly. Alesina, Devleeschauwer, Easterly, and Wacziarg (2003) developed new measures of ethnic, linguistic, and religious fractionalization for about 190 countries and used the data to estimate a negative impact of fractionalization on growth. Moreover, Aghion, Alesina, and Trebbi (2003) found that more ethnically fragmented societies have less-democratic political systems, and they interpreted this finding as suggesting that in more-fragmented societies the political system is chosen to insulate certain groups and to block the voice of others. But what is not clear from these empirical results is the political channels through which fragmentation affects growth. Further study is needed to identify these pathways of influence.

39. Parente and Prescott (2000) also argued that TFP differences across countries result from differences in entrenched interests that wield monopoly power (chap. 8), and from differences in regulatory constraints (chap. 6).

40. Olson (1982, chap. 4) also reported a negative correlation between the number of years of statehood of non-Confederate U.S. states and

their growth rates as evidence that the longer the stable environment, the slower the growth rate. In addition, he examined other countries in continental Europe, as well as Australia and New Zealand, for the effects of economic integration and trade policies on growth. And he studied a variety of historical cases of growth-restraining factions in Europe and other parts of the world.

41. Grossman and Helpman (2001) explored a host of generic mechanisms through which interest groups affect policies. Their analytical framework can be extended to the effects of interest groups on growth, but dynamic issues of this sort have so far received scant attention. Two examples of such an analysis are, however, provided by Krusell and Ríos-Rull (1996) and Grossman and Helpman (1998).

42. Electoral systems are complex, and they differ in many ways. The key distinction between proportional and majoritarian systems is, however, that in proportional systems representation is determined by the overall distribution of vote shares while in majoritarian systems representation is determined by the distribution of winners across districts. Presidential and parliamentary systems also have many variants, but a key distinction is that in presidential systems there is a strong separation of power between the executive and the legislature, while in parliamentary systems this separation is weak.

43. See Persson and Tabellini (2003, chap. 7).

44. These are Hall and Jones's (1999) indexes of antidiversion policies—that is, law and order, bureaucratic quality, corruption, risk of expropriation, and government repudiation of contracts.

45. Persson (2003) also provided time-series evidence on changes in regimes that corroborates the evidence from the cross-country variations.

46. See Chandler (1977) on the growth of large business corporations and the process of vertical integration, and Feenstra (1998) on the fragmentation of production.

# REFERENCES

Abramovitz, Moses. 1956. "Resource and Output Trends in the United States since 1870." *American Economic Review (Papers and Proceedings)* 46: 5–23.

Acemoglu, Daron. 1998. "Technical Change, Inequality, and the Labor Market." *Quarterly Journal of Economics* 113: 1055–89.

—— 2002a. "Why Do New Technologies Complement Skills? Directed Technical Change and Wage Inequality." *Journal of Economic Literature* 40: 7–72.

—— 2002b. "Directed Technical Change." *Review of Economic Studies* 69: 781–809.

—— 2003. "Patterns of Skill Premia." *Review of Economic Studies* 70: 199–230.

Acemoglu, Daron, Philippe Aghion, and Fabrizio Zilibotti. 2002. "Vertical Integration and Distance to Frontier." NBER Working Paper no. 9191.

—— 2003. "Distance to Frontier, Selection, and Economic Growth." Photocopy.

Acemoglu, Daron, and Joshua D. Angrist. 2001. "How Large Are the Social Returns to Education? Evidence from Compulsory Attendance Laws." *NBER Macroeconomic Annual 2001,* vol. 16, 9–59.

Acemoglu, Daron, and Simon Johnson. 2003. "Unbundling Institutions." NBER Working Paper no. 9934.

Acemoglu, Daron, Simon Johnson, and James A. Robinson. 2001. "The Colonial Origins of Comparative Development: An Empirical Investigation." *American Economic Review* 91: 1369–1401.

—— 2002. "Reversal of Fortune: Geography and Institutions in the Making of the Modern World Income Distribution." *Quarterly Journal of Economics* 117: 1231–94.

Acemoglu, Daron, and James A. Robinson. 2003. "Economic Origins of Dictatorship and Democracy." Manuscript. January.

Acemoglu, Daron, and Jaume Ventura. 2002. "The World Income Distribution." *Quarterly Journal of Economics* 117: 659–94.

Aghion, Philippe, Alberto Alesina, and Francesco Trebbi. 2003. "Endogenous Political Institutions." Photocopy.

Aghion, Philippe, Eve Caroli, and Cecilia García-Peñalosa. 1999. "Inequality and Economic Growth: The Perspective of the New Growth Theories." *Journal of Economic Literature* 37: 1615–60.

Aghion, Philippe, Christopher Harris, Peter Howitt, and John Vickers. 2001. "Competition, Imitation and Growth with Step-by-Step Innovation." *Review of Economic Studies* 68: 467–492.

Aghion, Philippe, and Peter Howitt. 1992. "A Model of Growth through Creative Destruction." *Econometrica* 60: 323–51.

—— Forthcoming. "Growth with Quality-Improving Innovations: An Integrated Framework." In Philippe Aghion and Steven N. Durlauf, eds., *Handbook of Economic Growth*. Amsterdam: Elsevier.

Alesina, Alberto, Arnaud Devleeschauwer, William Easterly, and Romain Wacziarg. 2003. "Fractionalization." *Journal of Economic Growth* 8: 155–194.

Alesina, Alberto, and Dani Rodrik. 1994. "Distribution Politics and Economic Growth." *Quarterly Journal of Economics* 109: 465–490.

Alesina, Alberto, Enrico Spolaore, and Romain Wacziarg. 2003. "Trade, Growth, and the Size of Countries." Harvard Institute for Economic Research Discussion Paper 1995.

Arrow, Kenneth J. 1962a. "The Economic Implications of Learning by Doing." *Review of Economic Studies* 29: 155–173.

—— 1962b. "Economic Welfare and the Allocation of Resources for Invention." In *The Rate of Return and Direction of Inventive Activity: Economic and Social Factors*. NBER Special Conference Series, vol. 13. Princeton: Princeton University Press.

—— 1974. *The Limits of Organization*. New York: W. W. Norton and Company.

Autor, David H., Lawrence F. Katz, and Alan B. Krueger. 1998. "Computing Inequality: Have Computers Changed the Labor Market?" *Quarterly Journal of Economics* 113: 1169–1213.

Bairoch, Paul. 1993. *Economics and World History*. Chicago: University of Chicago Press.

Banerjee, Abhijit V., and Esther Duflo. 2003. "Inequality and Growth: What Can the Data Say?" *Journal of Economic Growth* 8: 267–299.

Bardhan, Pranab K. 1970. *Economic Growth, Development, and Foreign Trade*. New York: Wiley.

Barro, Robert J. 1991. "Economic Growth in a Cross Section of Countries." *Quarterly Journal of Economics* 106: 407–443.

—— 1997. *Determinants of Economic Growth.* Cambridge: MIT Press.

—— "Inequality and Growth in a Panel of Countries." *Journal of Economic Growth* 5: 5–32.

Barro, Robert J., Gregory N. Mankiw, and Xavier Sala-i-Martin. 1995. "Capital Mobility in Neoclassical Models of Growth." *American Economic Review* 85: 103–115.

Barro, Robert J., and Xavier Sala-i-Martin. 1992. "Convergence." *Journal of Political Economy* 100: 223–258.

Baumol, William J., Sue Anne Batey Blackman, and Edward J. Wolff. 1989. *Productivity and American Leadership: The Long View* Cambridge: MIT Press.

Bayoumi, Tamim, David T. Coe, and Elhanan Helpman. 1999. "R&D Spillovers and Global Growth." *Journal of International Economics* 47: 399–428.

Beaudry, Paul, and David A. Green. 2003. "Wages and Employment in the United States and Germany: What Explains the Differences?" *American Economic Review* 93: 573–602.

Becker, Gary S., Kevin M. Murphy, and Robert Tamura. 1990. "Human Capital, Fertility, and Economic Growth." *Journal of Political Economy* 98: S12–S37.

Ben-David, Dan. 1993. "Equalizing Exchange: Trade Liberalization and Income Convergence." *Quarterly Journal of Economics* 108: 653–679.

Berman, Eli, John Bound, and Zvi Griliches. 1994. "Changes in the Demand for Skilled Labor in U.S. Manufacturing Industries: Evidence from the Annual Survey of Manufacturing." *Quarterly Journal of Economics* 109: 367–398.

Berman, Eli, John Bound, and Stephen Machin. 1998. "Implications of Skill-Biased Technological Change: International Evidence." *Quarterly Journal of Economics* 113: 1245–79.

Berman, Eli, and Stephen Machin. 2000. "Skill-Biased Technology Transfer: Evidence of Factor Biased Technological Change in Developing Countries." Photocopy.

Bernstein, Jeffrey I., and Pierre Mohnen. 1998. "International R&D Spillovers between U.S. and Japanese R&D Intensive Sectors." *Journal of International Economics* 44: 315–338.

Bhagwati, Jagdish. 1958. "Immiserizing Growth: A Geometric Note." *Review of Economic Studies* 25: 201–205.

Blomström, Magnus, Robert E. Lipsey, and Mario Zejan. 1996. "Is Fixed Investment the Key to Economic Growth?" *Quarterly Journal of Economics* 111: 269–276.

Booth, Alan, Joseph Melling, and Christoph Dartmann. 1997. "Institutions and Economic Growth: The Politics of Productivity in West Germany, Sweden, and the United Kingdom, 1945–1955." *Journal of Economic History* 57: 416–447.

Borjas, George J., Richard B. Freeman, and Lawrence F. Katz. 1997. "How Much Do Immigration and Trade Affect Labor Market Outcome?" *Brookings Papers on Economic Activity,* vol. 1, 1–90.

Botero, Juan, Simeon Djankov, Raphael La Porta, Florencio Lopez-de-Silanes, and Andrei Shleifer. 2003. "The Regulation of Labor." NBER Working Paper no. 9756.

Bourguignon, François. 1979. "Decomposable Income Inequality Measures." *Econometrica* 47: 901–920.

Bourguignon, François, and Christian Morrisson. 2002. "Inequality among World Citizens: 1820–1992." *American Economic Review* 92: 727–744.

Bresnahan, Timothy, and Manuel Trajtenberg. 1995. "General Purpose Technologies: 'Engines of Growth,'" *Journal of Econometrics* 65: 83–108.

Caselli, Francesco. 1999. "Technological Revolutions." *American Economic Review* 89: 78–102.

Caselli, Francesco, and Wilbur John Coleman II. 2001. "Cross-Country Technology Diffusion: The Case of Computers," *American Economic Review (Papers and Proceedings)* 91: 328–335.

—— 2003. "The World Technology Frontier." Photocopy. (Revised version of NBER Working Paper no. 7904, 2000.)

Caselli, Francesco, Gerardo Esquivel, and Fernando Lefort. 1996. "Reopening the Convergence Debate: A New Look at Cross-Country Growth Empirics." *Journal of Economic Growth* 1: 363–389.

Cass, David. 1965. "Optimum Growth in an Aggregative Model of Capital Accumulation." *Review of Economic Studies* 32: 223–240.

Chandler, Alfred D., Jr. 1977. *The Visible Hand.* Cambridge: Harvard University Press.

Clemens, Michael, and Jeffrey G. Williamson. 2002. "Why Did the Tariff-Growth Correlation Reverse after 1950?" NBER Working Paper no. 9181.

Coatsworth, John H. 1993. "Notes on the Comparative Economic History of Latin America and the United States." In Walther L. Bernecker and Hans Werner Tobler, eds., *Development and Underdevelopment in America.* New York: Walter de Gruyter.

Coe, David T., and Elhanan Helpman. 1995. "International R&D Spillovers." *European Economic Review* 39: 859–887.

Coe, David T., Elhanan Helpman, and Alexander W. Hoffmaister. 1997. "North-South R&D Spillovers." *Economic Journal* 107: 134–149.

Cohen, Daniel, and Marcelo Soto. 2001. "Growth and Human Capital:

Good Data, Good Results." Discussion Paper no. 3025, Centre for Economic Policy Research.

Conçeicão, Pedro, and Pedro Ferreira. 2000. "The Young Person's Guide to the Theil Index: Suggesting Intuitive Interpretations and Exploring Analytical Applications." UTIP Working Paper no. 14.

David, Paul. 1991. "Computer and Dynamo: The Modern Productivity Paradox in a Not-Too-Distant Mirror." In *Technology and Productivity: The Challenge for Economic Policy.* Paris: OECD.

Deininger, Klaus, and Lyn Squire. 1996. "Measuring Income Inequality: A New Data Base." *World Bank Economic Review* 10: 565–591.

—— 1998. "New Ways of Looking at Old Issues: Inequality and Growth." *Journal of Development Economics* 57: 259–287.

De Long, Bradford J., and Andrei Shleifer. 1993. "Princes and Merchants: European City Growth before the Industrial Revolution." *Journal of Law and Economics* 39: 671–702.

Desjonqueres, Thibaut, Stephen Machin, and John Van Reenen. 1999. "Another Nail in the Coffin? Or Can the Trade Based Explanation of Changing Skill Structures Be Resurrected?" *Scandinavian Journal of Economics* 101: 533–554.

DiNardo, John E., Nicole M. Fortin, and Thomas Lemieux. 1996. "Labor Market Institutions and the Distribution of Wages, 1973–1992: A Semi-Parametric Approach." *Econometrica* 64: 1001–44.

Dixit, Avinash. Forthcoming. *Lawlessness and Economics.* Princeton: Princeton University Press.

Djankov, Simeon, Edward L. Glaeser, Raphael La Porta, Florencio Lopez-de-Silanes, and Andrei Shleifer. 2003. "The New Comparative Economics." *Journal of Comparative Economics* 31: 595–619.

Djankov, Simeon, Raphael La Porta, Florencio Lopez-de-Silanes, and

Andrei Shleifer. 2002. "The Regulation of Entry." *Quarterly Journal of Economics* 117: 1–37.

—— 2003. "Courts." *Quarterly Journal of Economics* 118: 453–517.

Dollar, David. 1992. "Outward Oriented Developing Economies Really Do Grow More Rapidly: Evidence from 95 LDCs, 1976–1985." *Economic Development and Cultural Change* 40: 523–544.

Dollar, David, and Aart Kraay. 2002. "Growth Is Good for the Poor." *Journal of Economic Growth* 7: 195–225.

Du Boff, R. B. 1967. "The Introduction of Electric Power in American Manufacturing." *Economic History Review* 20: 509–518.

Durlauf, Steven N., and Danny T. Quah. 1999. "The New Empirics of Economic Growth." In John B. Taylor and Michael Woodford, eds., *Handbook of Macroeconomics,* vol. 1A. Amsterdam: Elsevier.

Dynan, Karen E., Jonathan Skinner, and Stephen P. Zeldes. Forthcoming. "Do the Rich Save More?" *Journal of Political Economy.*

Easterly, William, and Ross Levine. 2001. "It's Not Factor Accumulation: Stylized Facts and Growth Models." *World Bank Economic Review* 15: 177–219.

—— 2003. "Tropics, Germs, and Crops: How Endowments Influence Economic Development," *Journal of Monetary Economics* 50: 3–39.

Eaton, Jonathan, and Samuel Kortum. 1996. "Trade in Ideas: Patenting and Productivity in the OECD." *Journal of International Economics* 40: 251–278.

—— 1999. "International Technology Diffusion: Theory and Measurement." *International Economic Review* 40: 537–570.

Edwards, Sebastian. 1992. "Trade Orientation, Distortions, and Growth in Developing Countries." *Journal of Development Economics* 39: 31–57.

—— 1993. "Openness, Trade Liberalization, and Growth in Developing Countries." *Journal of Economic Literature* 31: 1358–93.

Engelbrecht, Hans-Juergen. 1997. "International R&D Spillovers, Human Capital, and Productivity in OECD Economies: An Empirical Investigation." *European Economic Review* 41: 1479–88.

Engerman, Stanley L., and Kenneth L. Sokoloff. 1997. "Factor Endowments, Institutions, and Differential Paths of Growth among New World Economies: A View from Economic Historians of the United States." In Stephen Haber, ed., *How Latin America Fell Behind.* Stanford: Stanford University Press.

Estevadeordal, Antoni, Brian Frantz, and Alan M. Taylor. 2003. "The Rise and Fall of World Trade: 1870–1939." *Quarterly Journal of Economics* 118: 359–407.

Fan, Emma X. 2002. "Technological Spillovers from Foreign Direct Investment—A Survey." Asian Development Bank, ERD Working Paper no. 33.

Feder, Gershon. 1982. "On Exports and Economic Growth." *Journal of Development Economics* 12: 59–73.

Feenstra, Robert C. 1998. "Integration of Trade and Disintegration of Production in the Global Economy." *Journal of Economic Perspectives* 12: 31–50.

Feenstra, Robert C., and Gordon H. Hanson. 1996. "Foreign Investment, Outsourcing, and Relative Wages," In Robert C. Feenstra, Gene M. Grossman, and Douglas A. Irwin, eds., *The Political Economy of Trade Policy: Papers in Honor of Jagdish Bhagwati.* Cambridge: MIT Press.

—— 1999. "Productivity Measurement and the Impact of Trade and Technology on Wages: Estimates for the U.S., 1972–1990." *Quarterly Journal of Economics* 114: 907–940.

—— 2003. "Global Production Sharing and Rising Inequality: A Survey of Trade and Wages," in Kwan Choi and James Harrigan, eds., *Handbook of International Trade.* New York: Basil Blackwell.

Forbes, Kristin J. 2000. "A Reassessment of the Relationship between Inequality and Growth." *American Economic Review* 90: 869–887.

Frankel, Jeffrey A., and David Romer. 1996. "Trade and Growth: An Empirical Investigation." NBER Working Paper no. 5476.

—— 1999. "Does Trade Cause Growth?" *American Economic Review* 89: 379–399.

Galor, Oded, and Tomer Moav. 2002. "Natural Selection and the Origin of Economic Growth." *Quarterly Journal of Economics* 117: 1133–91.

—— Forthcoming. "From Physical to Human Capital Accumulation: Inequality and the Process of Development." *Review of Economic Studies.*

Galor, Oded, and Andrew Mountford. 2003. "Trade, Demographic Transition, and the Great Divergence: Why Are a Third of People Indian and Chinese." Brown University, January 13. Photocopy.

Galor, Oded, and Daniel Tsiddon. 1997. "Technological Progress, Mobility, and Economic Growth." *American Economic Review* 87: 363–382.

Galor, Oded, and David N. Weil. 2000. "Population, Technology, and Growth: From the Malthusian Regime to the Demographic Transition." *American Economic Review* 90: 806–828.

Galor, Oded, and Joseph Zeira. 1993. "Income Distribution and Macroeconomics." *Review of Economic Studies* 60: 35–52.

Gawande, Kishore, and Pravin Krishna. 2003. "The Political Economy of Trade Policy: Empirical Approaches." in Kwan Choi and James Harrigan, eds., *Handbook of International Trade.* New York: Basil Blackwell.

Glaeser, Edward L., and Andrei Shleifer. 2002. "Legal Origins." *Quarterly Journal of Economics* 117: 1193–1229.

Goldberg, Penelopi K., and Giovanni Maggi. 1999. "Protection for Sale: An Empirical Investigation." *American Economic Review* 89: 833–850.

Goldin, Claudia, and Lawrence F. Katz. 1998. "The Origins of Technology-Skill Complementarity." *Quarterly Journal of Economics* 113: 693–732.

—— 2001. "The Legacy of U.S. Educational Leadership: Notes on Distribution and Economic Growth in the 20th Century." *American Economic Review (Papers and Proceedings)* 91: 18–23.

Gordon, Robert J. 2000. "Interpreting the 'One Big Wave' in U.S. Long-Term Productivity Growth." NBER Working Paper no. 7752.

Greenwood, Jeremy, Zvi Hercowitz, and Per Krusell. 1997. "Long-Run Implications of Investment-Specific Technological Change." *American Economic Review* 87: 342–362.

Greenwood, Jeremy, and Boyan Jovanovic. 1999. "The Information-Technology Revolution and the Stock Market." *American Economic Review (Papers and Proceedings)* 89: 116–122.

Greenwood, Jeremy, and Mehemet Yorokolgu. 1997. "1974." *Carnegie-Rochester Conference Series on Public Policy,* vol. 46, 49–95.

Greif, Avner. 1993. "Contract Enforceability and Economic Institutions in Early Trade: The Maghribi Traders' Coalition." *American Economic Review* 83: 525–548.

—— N.d. "Institutions: Theory and History." Manuscript.

Griffith, Rachel, Stephen Redding, and John Van Reenen. 2003. "R&D and Absorptive Capacity: Theory and Empirical Evidence." *Scandinavian Journal of Economics* 105: 99–118.

Griliches, Zvi. 1969. "Capital-Skill Complementarity." *Review of Economics and Statistics* 51: 465–468.

—— 1979. "Issues in Assessing the Contribution of Research and Development in Productivity Growth." *Bell Journal of Economics* 10: 92–116.

—— 1992. "The Search for R&D Spillovers." *Scandinavian Journal of Economics* 94: 29–47.

—— 2000. *R&D, Education, and Productivity.* Cambridge: Harvard University Press.

Grossman, Gene M., and Elhanan Helpman. 1991a. "Quality Ladders in the Theory of Growth." *Review of Economic Studies* 58: 43–61.

—— 1991b. *Innovation and Growth in the Global Economy.* Cambridge: MIT Press.

—— 1994a. "Endogenous Innovation in the Theory of Growth." *Journal of Economic Perspectives* 8: 23–44.

—— 1994b. "Protection for Sale." *American Economic Review* 84: 833–850.

—— 1995. "Technology and Trade." In Gene M. Grossman and Kenneth Rogoff, eds., *Handbook of International Economics,* vol. 3. Amsterdam: Elsevier.

—— 1996. "Electoral Competition and Special Interest Politics." *Review of Economic Studies* 63: 265–286.

—— 1998. "Intergenerational Redistribution with Short-lived Governments." *Economic Journal* 108: 1299–1329.

—— 2001. *Special Interest Politics.* Cambridge: MIT Press.

Hall, Robert E., and Charles I. Jones. 1999. "Why Do Some Countries Produce So Much More Output per Worker than Others?" *Quarterly Journal of Economics* 114: 83–116.

Hanushek, Eric, and Dennis D. Kimko. 2000. "Schooling, Labor-Force Quality, and the Growth of Nations." *American Economic Review* 90: 1184–1208.

Hejazi, Walid, and Edward A. Safarian. 1999. "Trade, Foreign Direct Investment, and R&D Spillovers." *Journal of International Business Studies* 30: 491–511.

Helpman, Elhanan, ed. 1998. *General Purpose Technologies and Economic Growth*. Cambridge: MIT Press.

Helpman, Elhanan, and Paul R. Krugman. 1985. *Market Structure and Foreign Trade*. Cambridge: MIT Press.

Helpman, Elhanan, and Antonio Rangel. 1999. "Adjusting to a New Technology: Experience and Training." *Journal of Economic Growth.* 4: 359–383.

Helpman, Elhanan, and Manuel Trajtenberg. 1998. "A Time to Sow and a Time to Reap: Growth Based on General Purpose Technologies." In Elhanan Helpman, ed., *General Purpose Technologies and Economic Growth*. Cambridge: MIT Press.

Hornstein, Andreas, and Per Krusell. 1996. "Can Technology Improvements Cause Productivity Slowdowns?" *NBER Macroeconomic Annual 1996,* vol. 11, 209–259.

Howitt, Peter. 1999. "Steady State Growth with Population and R&D Inputs Growing." *Journal of Political Economy* 107: 715–730.

—— 2000. "Endogenous Growth and Cross-Country Income Differences." *American Economic Review* 90: 829–846.

Huntington, Samuel P. 1968. *Political Order in Changing Societies.* New Haven: Yale University Press.

IMF. 2001. *World Economic Outlook: October 2001.* Washington, DC: IMF.

Irwin, Douglas A., and Peter J. Klenow. 1994. "Learning by Doing Spillovers in the Semiconductor Industry," *Journal of Political Economy* 102: 1200–27.

Irwin, Douglas A., and Marko Terviö. 2002. "Does Trade Raise Income?

Evidence from the Twentieth Century." *Journal of International Economics* 58: 1–18.

Islam, Nazrul. 1995. "Growth Empirics: A Panel Data Approach." *Quarterly Journal of Economics* 110: 1127–70.

—— 2001. "Different Approaches to Comparison of Total Factor Productivity." In Charles R. Hulten, Edwin R. Dean, and Michael J. Harper, eds., *New Developments in Productivity Analysis*. Chicago: University of Chicago Press.

Jaffe, Adam B., and Manuel Trajtenberg. 2002. *Patents, Citations, and Innovations*. Cambridge: MIT Press.

Jones, Charles I. 1995a. "Time Series Tests of Endogenous Growth Models." *Quarterly Journal of Economics* 110: 495–525.

—— 1995b. "R&D-Based Models of Economic Growth." *Journal of Political Economy* 103: 759–784.

—— 1997. "On the Evolution of the World Income Distribution," *Journal of Economic Perspectives* 11: 19–36.

—— 2002. "Sources of U.S. Economic Growth in a World of Ideas." *American Economic Review* 92: 220–239.

Jones, Larry E., and Rodolfo E. Manuelli. 1990. "A Convex Model of Equilibrium Growth: Theory and Policy Implications." *Journal of Political Economy* 98: 1008–38.

Jorgenson, Dale W. 2001. "Information Technology and the U.S. Economy." *American Economic Review* 91: 1–32.

—— N.d. "Information Technology and the G7 Economies." Harvard University. Photocopy.

Jorgenson, Dale W., and Zvi Griliches. 1967. "The Explanation of Productivity Change." *Review of Economic Studies* 34: 249–283.

Jorgenson, Dale W., and Eric Yip. 2001. "Whatever Happened to Productivity Growth?" In Charles R. Hulten, Edwin R. Dean, and Michael J. Harper, eds., *New Developments in Productivity Analysis.* Chicago: University of Chicago Press.

Kaldor, Nicholas. 1955–56. "Alternative Theories of Distribution." *Review of Economic Studies* 23: 94–100.

Katz, Larry F., and David H. Autor. 1999. "Changes in the Wage Structure and Earnings Inequality." In Orley C. Ashenfelter and David Card, eds., *Handbook of Labor Economics,* vol. 3A. Amsterdam: Elsevier.

Katz, Larry F., and Kevin M. Murphy. 1992. "Changes in Relative Wages, 1963–1987: Supply and Demand Factors." *Quarterly Journal of Economics* 107: 35–78.

Keller, Wolfgang. 1998. "Are International R&D Spillovers Trade-Related? Analyzing Spillovers among Randomly Marched Trade Partners." *European Economic Review* 42: 1469–81.

—— 2001. "Knowledge Spillovers at the World's Technology Frontier." Discussion Paper no. 2815, CEPR.

Khan, Zonina B., and Kenneth L. Sokolott. 2001. "The Early Development of Intellectual Property Institutions in the United States." *Journal of Economic Perspectives* 15: 233–246.

King, Robert G., and Sergio T. Rebelo. 1993. "Transitional Dynamics and Economic Growth in the Neoclassical Model." *American Economic Review* 83: 908–931.

Klenow, Peter J., and Andrés Rodríguez-Clare. 1997. "The Neoclassical Revival in Growth Economics: Has It Gone Too Far?" *NBER Macroeconomics Annual 1997,* vol. 12, 73–103.

Knack, Stephen, and Philip Keefer. 1995. "Institutions and Economic Performance: Cross-Country Tests Using Alternative Measures." *Economics and Politics* 7: 207–227.

Kremer, Michael. 1993. "Population Growth and Technological Change: One Million B.C. to 1990." *Quarterly Journal of Economics* 107: 681–716.

Krueger, Alan B., and Mikael Lindahl. 2001. "Education for Growth: Why and for Whom?" *Journal of Economic Literature* 39: 1101–36.

Krueger, Anne O. 1968. "Factor Endowments and Per Capita Income Differences among Countries." *Economic Journal* 78: 641–659.

Krugman, Paul R. 1987. "The Narrow Moving Band, the Dutch Disease, and the Competitive Consequences of Mrs. Thatcher: Notes on Trade in the Presence of Dynamic Scale Economies," *Journal of Development Economics* 27: 41–55.

—— 1994. "The Myth of Asia's Miracle." *Foreign Affairs* 73: 62–78.

—— 1995. "Growing World Trade: Causes and Consequences." *Brookings Papers on Economic Activity,* vol. 1, 327–362.

—— 2000. "Technology, Trade, and Factor Prices." *Journal of International Economics* 50: 51–72.

Krusell, Per, Lee E. Ohanian, José-Victor Ríos-Rull, and Giovanni L. Violante. 2000. "Capital-Skill Complementarity and Inequality: A Macroeconomic Analysis." *Econometrica* 68: 1029–53.

Krusell, Per, and José-Victor Ríos-Rull. 1996. "Vested Interests in a Positive Theory of Stagnation and Growth." *Review of Economic Studies* 63: 301–329.

Kuznets, Simon. 1955a. "Economic Growth and Income Inequality." *American Economic Review* 45: 1–28.

—— 1955b. "Quantitative Aspects of the Economic Growth of Nations: VIII. Distribution and Income by Size." *Economic Development and Cultural Change* 12: 1–80.

Kuznets, Simon. 1966. *Modern Economic Growth.* New Haven: Yale University Press.

Landes, David S. 1969. *The Unbound Prometheus.* Cambridge: Cambridge University Press.

—— 1998. *The Wealth and Poverty of Nations.* New York: W. W. Norton and Company.

Lane, Philip R., and Gian Maria Milesi-Ferretti. 2001. "The External Wealth of Nations: Measures of Foreign Assets and Liabilities for Industrial and Developing Countries." *Journal of International Economics* 55: 263–294.

La Porta, Rafael, Florencio Lopez-de-Silanes, Andrei Shleifer, and Robert W. Vishny. 1998. "Law and Finance." *Journal of Political Economy* 106: 1113–55.

—— 1994. "The Quality of Government." *Journal of Law, Economics, and Organization* 15: 222–279.

Lawrence, Robert, and Matthew J. Slaughter. 1993. "International Trade and American Wages in the 1980s: Giant Sucking Sound or Small Hiccup?" *Brookings Papers on Economic Activity,* vol. 1, 161–226.

Leamer, Edward E. 1988. "Measures of Openness." In Robert E. Baldwin, ed., *Trade Policy Issues and Empirical Analysis.* Chicago: University of Chicago Press.

—— 1998. "In Search of Stolper-Samuelson Linkages between International Trade and Lower Wages." In Susan M. Collins, ed., *Imports, Exports, and the American Worker.* Washington, D.C.: Brookings Institution Press.

—— 2000. "What's the Use of Factor Content?" *Journal of International Economics* 50: 17–50.

Levine, Ross, and David Renelt. 1992. "A Sensitivity Analysis of Cross-Country Growth Regressions." *American Economic Review* 82: 942–963.

Lichtenberg, Frank R., and Bruno van Pottelsberghe de la Potterie. 1998.

"International R&D Spillovers: A Comment." *European Economic Review* 42: 1483–91.

Lindert, Peter H., and Jeffrey G. Williamson. 1985. "Growth, Equality and History." *Explorations in Economic History* 22: 341–377.

Lipset, Seymour M. 1959. "Some Social Requisites of Democracy: Economic Development and Political Legitimacy." *American Political Science Review* 53: 69–105.

Lipsey, Richard G., Cliff Bekar, and Kenneth Carlaw. 1998. "What Requires Explanation?" In Elhanan Helpman, ed., *General Purpose Technologies and Economic Growth*. Cambridge: MIT Press.

Lockwood, William W. 1954. *The Economic Development of Japan: Growth and Structural Change, 1868–1938*. Princeton: Princeton University Press.

Lucas, Robert E., Jr. 1988. "On the Mechanics of Economic Development." *Journal of Monetary Economics* 22: 3–42.

——— 1990. "Why Doesn't Capital Flow from Rich to Poor Countries?" *American Economic Review (Papers and Proceedings)* 80: 92–96.

——— 2002. *Lectures on Economic Growth*. Cambridge: Harvard University Press.

Lundberg, Mattias, and Lyn Squire. 2003. "The Simultaneous Evolution of Growth and Inequality." *Economic Journal* 113: 326–344.

Maddison, Angus.1979. "Per Capita Output in the Long Run." *Kyklos* 32: 412–429.

——— 1982. *Phases of Capitalist Development*. New York: Oxford University Press.

——— 1995. *Monitoring the World Economy: 1820–1992*. Paris: OECD.

——— 2001. *The World Economy: A Millennial Perspective*. Paris: OECD.

Mankiw, N. Gregory. 1995. "The Growth of Nations." *Brookings Papers on Economic Activity*, vol. 1, 275–326.

Mankiw, N. Gregory, David Romer, and David N. Weil. 1992. "A Contribution to the Empirics of Economic Growth." *Quarterly Journal of Economics* 107: 407–438.

Marshall, Alfred. 1920. *Principles of Economics*. 8th ed. London: Macmillan.

Matsuyama, Kiminori. 1992. "Agricultural Productivity, Comparative Advantage, and Economic Growth." *Journal of Economic Theory* 58: 317–334.

Mauro, Paulo. 1995. "Corruption and Growth." *Quarterly Journal of Economics* 110: 681–712.

Mitch, David. 2001. "The Rise of Mass Education and Its Contribution to Economic Growth in Europe, 1800–2000." Prepared for the Fourth European Historical Economics Society Conference, Merton College, Oxford.

Mitra, Daveshin, Dimitrios D. Thomakos, and Mehmet A. Ulubaşoğlu. 2002. "'Protection for Sale' in a Developing Country: Democracy versus Dictatorship." *Review of Economics and Statistics* 84: 497–508.

Mohnen, Pierre. 1992. *The Relation between R&D and Productivity Growth in Canada and Other Major Industrial Countries*. Ottawa: Economic Council of Canada.

—— 1996. "R&D Externalities and Productivity Growth." *STI Review*, no. 18, 39–66.

Mokyr, Joel. 1990. *The Lever of Riches*. New York: Oxford University Press.

—— 2002. *The Gifts of Athena*. Princeton: Princeton University Press.

Moretti, Enrico. 2002. "Estimating the Social Return to Higher Education: Evidence from Longitudinal and Repeated Cross-Sectional Data." NBER Working Paper no. 9108.

Mulligan, Casey, and Xavier Sala-i-Martin. 1993. "Transitional Dynamics in Two-Sector Models of Economic Growth." *Quarterly Journal of Economics* 108: 739–773.

—— 2003. "Do Democracies Have Different Public Policies than Nondemocracies?" NBER Working Paper no. 10040.

North, Douglass C. 1981. *Structure and Change in Economic History.* New York: W. W. Norton and Company.

—— 1990. *Institutions, Institutional Change, and Economic Performance.* Cambridge: Cambridge University Press.

North, Douglass C., William Summerhill, and Barry R. Weingast. 2000. "Order, Disorder, and Economic Change: Latin America versus North America." In Bruce Bueno de Mesquita and Hilton Root, eds., *Governing for Prosperity.* New Haven: Yale University Press.

Olson, Mancur. 1965. *The Logic of Collective Action.* Cambridge: Harvard University Press.

—— 1982. *The Rise and Decline of Nations.* New Haven: Yale University Press.

O'Rourke, Kevin. 2000. "Tariffs and Growth in the Late 19th Century." *Economic Journal* 110: 456–483.

O'Rourke, Kevin, and Jeffrey G. Williamson. 1999. *Globalization and History: The Evolution of a Nineteenth Century Atlantic Economy.* Cambridge: MIT Press.

Parente, Stephen L., and Edward C. Prescott. 2000. *Barriers to Riches.* Cambridge: MIT Press.

Paukert, Felix. 1973. "Income Distribution at Different Levels of Development: A Survey of Evidence." *International Labor Review* 108: 97–125.

Perotti, Roberto. 1996. "Growth, Income Distribution, and Democracy: What the Data Say." *Journal of Economic Growth* 1: 149–187.

Persson, Torsten. 2003. "Consequences of Constitutions." Presidential Address, European Economic Association.

Persson, Torsten, and Guido Tabellini. 1992. "Growth, Distribution, and Politics." *European Economic Review* 36: 593–602.

—— 1994. "Is Inequality Harmful for Growth?" *American Economic Review* 84: 600–621.

—— 2003. *The Economic Effects of Constitutions.* Cambridge: MIT Press.

Piketty, Thomas. 1997. "The Dynamics of the Wealth Distribution and the Interest Rate with Credit Rationing." *Review of Economic Studies* 64: 173–189.

Pomeranz, Kenneth. 2000. *The Great Divergence.* Princeton: Princeton University Press.

Przeworski, Adam, Michael E. Alvarez, José Antonio Cheibub, and Fernando Limongi. 2000. *Democracy and Development.* Cambridge: Cambridge University Press.

Psacharopoulos, George. 1994. "Returns to Investment in Education: A Global Update." *World Development* 22: 1325–43.

Quah, Danny. 2002. "One Third of the World's Growth and Inequality." CEPR Discussion Paper no. 3316.

Ravallion, Martin, and Shaohua Chen. 1997. "What Can New Survey Data Tell Us about Recent Changes in Distribution and Poverty." *World Bank Economic Review* 11: 357–382.

Rodríguez, Francisco, and Dani Rodrik. 2000. "Trade Policy and Economic Growth: A Skeptic's Guide to the Cross-National Evidence." *NBER Macroeconomic Annual 2000,* vol. 15, 261–325.

Rodrik, Dani. 1999. "Democracies Pay Higher Wages." *Quarterly Journal of Economics* 114: 707–738.

Rodrik, Dani, Arvind Subramanian, and Francesco Trebbi. 2002. "Institutions Rule: The Primacy of Institutions over Geography and Integration in Economic Development." NBER Working Paper no. 9305.

Rogowski, Ronald. 1989. *Commerce and Coalitions*. Princeton: Princeton University Press.

Romer, Paul M. 1986. "Increasing Returns and Long-Run Growth." *Journal of Political Economy* 94: 1002–37.

—— 1990. "Endogenous Technological Change." *Journal of Political Economy* 98: S71–S102.

Rosenberg, Nathan. 1982. *Inside the Black Box*. Cambridge: Cambridge University Press.

Rosenberg, Nathan and L. E. Birdzell, Jr. 1986. *How the West Grew Rich*. New York: Basic Books.

Ruiz-Arranz, Marta. N.d. "Wage Inequality and Information Technology in the U.S." Harvard University. Photocopy.

Sachs, Jeffrey D. 2001. "Tropical Underdevelopment." NBER Working Paper no. 8119.

Sachs, Jeffrey D., and Andrew Warner. 1995. "Economic Reform and the Process of Global Integration." *Brookings Papers on Economic Activity*, vol. 1, 1–118.

Sala-i-Martin, Xavier. 2002. "The World Distribution of Income (Estimated from Individual Country Distributions)." NBER Working Paper no. 8933.

Scherer, Frederic M. 1982. "Inter-Industry Technology Flows and Productivity Growth." *Review of Economics and Statistics* 64: 627–634.

Schmidt-Hebbel, Klaus, and Luis Serven. 2000. "Does Income Inequality

Raise Aggregate Saving?" *Journal of Development Economics* 61: 417–446.

Schott, Peter K. 2003. "One Size Fits All? Heckscher-Ohlin Specialization in Global Production." *American Economic Review* 93: 686–708.

Schumpeter, Joseph. 1942. *Capitalism, Socialism, and Democracy.* New York: Harper and Row.

Segerstrom, Paul S. 1998. "Endogenous Growth without Scale Effects." *American Economic Review* 88: 1290–1310.

Segerstrom, Paul S., T. C. A. Anant, and Elias Dinopoulos. 1990. "A Schumpeterian Model of the Product Life Cycle." *American Economic Review* 80: 1077–92.

Shell, Karl. 1967. "A Model of Inventive Activity and Capital Accumulation." In Karl Shell, ed., *Essays on the Theory of Optimal Economic Growth.* Cambridge: MIT Press.

Slaughter, Matthew J. 2000. "What Are the Results of Product-Price Studies and What Can We Learn from Their Differences?" In Feenstra, Robert C., ed., *The Effects of International Trade on Wages.* Chicago: University of Chicago Press.

Sokoloff, Kenneth L., and Stanley L. Engerman. 2000. "Institutions, Factor Endowments, and Paths of Development in the New World." *Journal of Economic Perspectives* 14: 217–232.

Solow, Robert M. 1956. "A Contribution to the Theory of Economic Growth." *Quarterly Journal of Economics* 70: 65–94.

Solow, Robert M. 1957. "Technical Change and the Aggregate Production Function." *Review of Economics and Statistics* 39: 312–320.

Stolper, Wolfgang F., and Paul A. Samuelson. 1941. "Protection and Real Wages." *Review of Economic Studies* 9: 58–73.

Summers, Robert, and Alan Heston. 1991. "The Penn World Table (Mark

5): An Expanded Set of International Comparisons, 1950–1988."
*Quarterly Journal of Economics* 106: 327–368.

Terleckyj, Nester E. 1980. "Direct and Indirect Effects of Industrial Research and Development on the Productivity Growth of Industries." In John W. Kendrick and Beatrice N. Vaccara, eds., *New Developments in Productivity Measurement and Analysis.* Chicago: University of Chicago Press.

Trefler, Daniel, and Susan Chun Zhu. 2001. "Ginis in General Equilibrium: Trade, Technology, and Southern Inequality." NBER Working Paper no. 8446.

Uzawa, Hirofumi. 1965. "Optimum Technical Change in an Aggregative Model of Economic Growth." *International Economic Review* 6: 18–31.

Ventura, Jaume. 1997. "Growth and Interdependence." *Quarterly Journal of Economics* 112: 57–84.

von Tunzelmann, Nick G. 1978. *Steam Power and British Industrialization in 1860.* Oxford: Clarendon Press.

Wacziarg, Romain. 2001. "Measuring the Dynamic Gains from Trade." *World Bank Economic Review* 15: 393–429.

Wood, Adrian. 1994. *North-South Trade, Employment, and Inequality: Changing Fortunes in a Skill Driven World.* Oxford: Clarendon Press.

Young, Alwyn. 1992. "A Tale of Two Cities: Factor Accumulation and Technical Change in Hong Kong and Singapore." *NBER Macroeconomic Annual 1992,* vol. 7, 13–54.

—— 1995. "The Tyranny of Numbers: Confronting the Statistical Realities of the East Asian Growth Experience." *Quarterly Journal of Economics* 110: 641–680.

—— 1998. "Growth without Scale Effects." *Journal of Political Economy* 106: 41–63.

# INDEX